God's Special Children

God's Special Children

Helping the Handicapped Achieve

Keith J. Karren
Sherrie A. Hundley

INTERNATIONAL STANDARD BOOK NUMBER
0-88290-086-2

Printed in the
United States of America
by
Horizon Publishers
& Distributors
P.O. Box 490
50 South 500 West
Bountiful, Utah 84010

Preface

As we travel through life, we sometimes see something which touches us deeply and gives special meaning to our existence. That something—or someone—creates within us a feeling that only we ourselves can evaluate. It can bring smiles, or tears, happiness or heartache, joy or regret. Either way, that feeling is often something we need to share with someone.

We have been touched by special experiences of this kind and it is our desire to share them with others, that they may bring encouragement and hope to those who may find themselves faced with a handicap in some form or another.

Everyone has handicaps. They may be called faults or weaknesses or flaws, but the handicaps are there, in all of us, even though they may not always show. They may not come in the form of a crippled leg, or blindness, or an under-developed mind, but few of us manage to escape being affected in some way with physical or mental disabilities. And the Bible tells us, "For we know that the whole creation groaneth and travaileth in pain together." (Romans 8:22)

Michael was a healthy, normal, active child until stricken with polio at the age of two, which left him paralyzed from the waist down. Through meeting devastating challenges, he found a beautiful parent-child relationship and a happy life. Margaret was born with birth defects affecting every limb in her body. Her struggle to convince the world that she could be a productive human being brings profound insight to readers of her story. David was mentally retarded, but was endowed with special abilities to show love. Jim was tragically injured at the age of fourteen—the destruction of vital brain cells turning him into a "vegetable." Only through the constant love and care of his family was he able to regain most of his abilities, only to die unexpectedly while serving a mission for his church. His story is presented in the hope of showing that, in spite of the unexplained reason for his death, there was a definite reason for his life and the exemplary way that he lived it.

Can we learn anything from the Mikes, the Margarets, the Davids, the Jims, and others like them? We think so. Perhaps it is in the knowing of the trials of others that we ourselves are able to meet ours.

Charles Clayton Morrison adequately describes it in these words:

If it were not that we are all bound together in human suffering, I suppose no one of us would be able to face the griefs, the disappointments, the failures, the frustrations, denials of hope which life brings. You suffer, and I suffer, too. If I see you gallantly bearing your cross, I am reproached for my weakness, my whimpering, my stubborn irreconsibility. It is your way of meeting your grief that gives me heart to meet mine. It is the fact that some men and women walk so bravely into the shadow and come out with radiant faces—it is this fact that gives the rest of us courage when our turn comes. [1]

Whether or not your turn has come, we share with you these thoughts and stories with the hope that they may provide a meaningful experience in life. We hope that they may help us all to be more aware of our brother and his problem, and that they may give each of us a stronger desire to support him in his sorrow or need. The scriptures tell us that we should be willing to bear one another's burdens, that we should mourn with those who mourn and comfort those who stand in need of comfort.

May we all remember that no matter how difficult our trials, our weaknesses or our handicaps may be, God has given us a promise. "Peace be unto thy soul; thine adversity and thine afflictions shall be but a small moment; And then, if thou endure it well, God shall exalt thee on high; thou shalt triumph over all thy foes. (D & C 121:7-8)

Acknowledgments

It is our sincere desire to express gratitude to all those who have contributed in any way toward the publishing of this book.

First of all, we wish to thank those special people who have so willingly shared with us their inspiring stories: Mike Johnson; Lorna Simper, Margaret Van Noy; Dennis Dean; Steven Anderson; Charles and Christine Parkin and their daughter, Susan LeBaron; Richard Moore; Maurice Bowman, Jr.; Jim and Louise Baird, and their daughter, Janet; Neldon and Marilyn Stanley; Glen and Betty Brown and their son, Mike; Stan and Vicki Taylor and their son, Johnny; Beatrice Kingsley and her son, Dennis; Eslie and Gwen Christensen; William and Vera Hundley, and four others whom we will name later.

We also wish to convey our love and appreciation to our families, who have not only shared with us the joys and sorrows of life, but have given us their loving support in our joint effort to present the stories of some of God's Special Children.

To Diane, a helpful and understanding wife, and to Scott, Holli, Jamie Todd and Brady Karren, we extend our deepest thanks for sharing their Dad's time with the development of this book.

To John (many know him as "Jack"), a patient and encouraging husband, and to Eric, Paul, Dale and Steven Hundley, we also wish to express our gratitude, not only for their continued faith in the accomplishment of this writing, but for the concern they always showed to their beloved son and brother, David, as well as to other handicapped children.

I (Sherrie Hundley), would also like to pay tribute to my parents, Dwane and Grace Ahlstrom, for their encouragement and faith in me, and for the undying devotion they have demonstrated for many years toward the care and concern of my handicapped child, as well as my four other sons and foster daughter. I am also grateful to my mother-in-law, Lola Hundley, whose kindness, help and cheerful example have taught me many valuable lessons.

We both wish to express our thanks to Duane Crowther and his staff at Horizon Publishers for the helpful suggestions we have received in preparing this manuscript, and to our many friends and relatives who have shown a genuine interest in our work.

Our expression of appreciation would not be complete without thanks to Ora Pate Stewart for graciously allowing us to use three of her beautiful poems, which will also appear in her forthcoming book, *Summer Silver, Autumn Gold*.

And last of all, but most importantly, we dedicate this book to four special people: David Hundley, Don Hundley, Jim Christensen and Merrill Stanley, for it was through a desire to tell others of their exceptional ability to generate love that this book came to be. Now free of their "thorn in the flesh," they have passed on into another life, leaving behind them a loving memory and a great example for us all to follow.

Table of Contents

SECTION I — THE PARENTS SPEAK

caps are some of the greatest roadblocks in our society and she set out early in life to prove that having definite goals and working constantly toward them can produce unbelievable accomplishments.

SECTION III — RAISING A HANDICAPPED CHILD

Parents of a child who is pronounced as having a defect or handicap, go through typical stages of reaction and adjustment. An understanding of these normal reactions will help parents move through this transitory period and help their child and the family successfully adjust.

There are an estimated fifteen million Americans whose lives are affected by birth defects. A knowledge of how to prevent certain defects, as well as how to be a successful parent to a handicapped child, is discussed.

The key to helping the handicapped is to know the purpose of life itself. The purpose of life is tied to the religious experience of man. This chapter explores the differing religious philosophies of where the handicapped fit into the plan of God.

Knowledge is power. Nowhere is this more evident than when a family is hit with a birth defect or some kind of physical or mental handicap. Seeking help from known, professional sources can make the difference between success or failure. Lists of handicapping disorders and names of corresponding professional "help" organizations are given.

The bibliography lists outstanding books in the birth defect and handicapped area, with comments about the content of many of them. There are also several books listed for their inspirational qualities in helping us all to meet our problems in life.

Section One

The Parents Speak

When the great oak is straining in the wind,
The boughs drink in new beauty, and the trunk
Sends down a deeper root along the windward side.

Only the soul that knows a mighty grief
Can know a mighty rapture. Sorrows come
To stretch our spaces in the heart for joy.

—Edwin Markham

*W*hat do parents do when they learn that, though their beautiful little boy appears to be the child of their dreams, he is mentally retarded? When this happened to John and Sherrie Hundley, they were hardly prepared for such an experience. Having been married only a short time, they were looking forward to having a family, and had high hopes and desires for each child with which they might be blessed.

When they first learned that their son, David, was to live his life as a handicapped person, it was unbelievable—a disaster in their lives. They struggled with the uncertainty—the disappointments, and searched for answers, both medically and emotionally. Over the years they finally reached the point of acceptance of their son's abnormality, and in time, came to realize that his condition was not merely an incurable problem with which they must cope, but also a rich blessing in the family, because of the great love which they had for David and he had for them.

Their other children have also felt the glow of David's presence. He is no longer with them, but they feel that he is now fulfilling a measure of creation which he was unable to do here. The Hundleys have experienced much sorrow over David's condition, but now see that this need not necessarily be so. David's story is presented with the hope that others may also see that blessings often come in disguise, and that sometimes the richest blessings are found in the experiences which seem the most difficult to bear. The story is told by his mother.

Chapter 1

David Means Beloved

Story Of David Hundley

*A sunbeam quickly flashes through the sky
And then is gone,
The world a lighter place
        The day a brighter day,
For it was here.*

*A soul makes earth a visit brief
And then returns.
Pain a little sharper,
        Awareness greater still,
And love....
For he was here.*

—Unknown

This is the story of David—a boy who came into this world because he was wanted. And even though he was not what the world calls "normal," he was loved, from the moment he was born until he died, and even after his death. The name David means beloved.

I don't really know why we loved our David so deeply, unless it was because he needed so much to be loved, and in his sweet, undemanding way brought out that kind of love in us. Perhaps

17

this was his special calling, his purpose in this world, his gift from God.

Before David's birth, and even when he did not begin to develop as most children do, I gave little thought to the many "handicapped" people in the world.

David was our first child. I had a normal pregnancy with no indications whatsoever that anything might be wrong. My obstetrician was a man in whom I had every confidence. His knowledge and ability have long since proved that my faith in him was justified, and I will always think of him as a special friend.

David came into the world on February 25, 1956, three days before the expected arrival. Everything appeared to be normal, but in the actual delivery there was some difficulty and the doctor found it necessary to use instruments to help the situation along.

"It's a fine big boy," the doctor said when it was over. Eight pounds of boy, we later learned. Since nothing had been used but local anesthetics, I was wheeled out into the hall to tell my husband that he had the son for which he had hoped. Later he came to my room and said, "We'll name him David, because you've always wanted a David, and Dwane after your father." So it was David Dwane.

My heart was too full to express the feelings I had, but any young mother having the beautiful little baby she has always wanted would know what those feelings were. The hopes and dreams one has for such a child are unlimited. I didn't necessarily want him to become great or famous, but I hoped that he would have a good, happy life and possibly accomplish a little good in the world. I had prayed often that he would be normal: "Please, God, just let my baby be normal." But evidently, that was not to be.

When David was six days old, we took him home from the hospital. We were so happy and proud of our little son. Our relatives, neighbors and friends all came to see him and to express their joy for us. We took movies and showered him with love and kisses, toys and clothes. Everything was going along wonderfully. I remember I would sit and hold him and look at his dark hair and big, blue eyes and I would think to myself, "He's everything I ever wanted." Little did I know what was in store.

It was not until David was about six months old that we really suspected anything was wrong. As conscientious and anxious young parents, we realized that our little boy was not sitting up well. We had to support his back when we held him or he would fall backward. Later, we noticed that he did not put things into his mouth, as babies do, and that he didn't ever reach for things, even though he was always alert and seemed very happy.

Our pediatrician told us he was just a little slow, and the examinations showed David to be in excellent health. There were times, however, that I would get the feeling I would not always have him, and I did not know why. I had strong feelings that I should just enjoy every moment that I could with him.

We watched, prayed and cared for our son the best way we knew how. His father was very loving and attentive and all our relatives were concerned about him. A special blessing was given to him by our bishop, and we tried hard to exercise all the faith we could. We felt that things would work out all right in time, for we could see that he was a very special child and we loved him more each day.

People would say, "Oh, there can't be anything wrong with *that* beautiful child—he's so bright and alert and has such a great smile!" How I loved those precious days with my baby. He seldom cried and I enjoyed the time I could spend rocking him and singing to him. I am so grateful now for the pleasant memories of his early childhood. Those recollections are of great consolation to me now and I realize that we must grasp every thread of joy that we can from those cherished moments. Oh, how they fill my heart with pleasure in these later years when things are so different and I have no more babies. In the rush of life, we must never let these experiences pass us by, for they will be gone forever.

The happiness that we enjoyed with our new baby was soon changed. As I could not explain my feelings at David's birth, neither could I explain the feelings of deep despair which came to me after we had visited a specialist and were told the heart-breaking facts about David. I think the doctor tried to ease us into the realization of what he knew. There was a series of tests and examinations, and when I asked him what the diagnosis was, he replied without hesitation, *"symmetrical mental retardation."* It hit me like a shock of electricity! We had known David was not quite like other babies his age, that he was a little slow in developing, but my mind could not really comprehend the finality of the doctor's statement. I kept saying to myself, "please don't let it be true!"

It was difficult to understand how they could know that he would be retarded. The X-ray of his skull and upper body were normal. Electro-encephalograms (brain wave tests) showed no abnormalities. Blood test results were also normal. Psychological tests showed only slower development than usual, but no definite problems. The only thing they found of any consequence was that he had soft connective tissues. They said this could be the reason for his being slow to walk. Yet now we had to face the fact that he was going to be mentally retarded. The doctor was very definite about it. At the time, I thought he was being very cruel, but now I see that he was actually very kind in telling us what he did.

After the knowledge of his handicap began to sink in a little, we asked the doctor what we should do, silently hoping he would write a prescription or perhaps even suggest an operation which would cure the dreaded problem. There was no such advice. "Just take him home and love him," the doctor replied. I have wondered if this is a standard answer that doctors give to all parents of the retarded, as I have heard others say that they were told the same.

Learning of David's condition was the first real sorrow I had known, and I wondered how I could ever live with it. I later read that there is a blessing sent from God in every burden of sorrow and so I knew that I must look for it. Since then there have been other sorrows come into our lives, and I realize that in many ways our lives were enriched by having had David. I know that there was a purpose for David's life, just as there is for anyone who comes into this world. David actually realized very little about the activities that went on around him, yet he was aware of the fact that people cared about him and, in his limited way, was able to give something in return.

Should We Have More Children?

The doctor had said, "There is no reason to believe that David's problem is hereditary. It was just something that happened—an accident. The best thing to do is to have some more children." So our family began to grow. I see now that even from the time we learned of David's disability, I was greatly blessed. People have said, "Weren't you afraid to have another baby?" Somehow I had a calm and comforting feeling that everything would be all right, and it was. Our second son, Eric, was healthy, happy and normal. He and David loved each other very much and played together well. They were very special boys, each in his own way.

Our neighbor children would come and ask to play with David just as they would Eric. David could not run with them or ride bikes or climb trees, but he had that beautiful smile for everyone, along with a special sweetness about him which made everyone enjoy being near him.

As Eric grew and developed he brought a great deal of joy to us so that much of our grief over David's condition was dispelled. We went on living, as much as possible, as we had planned. David was treated like a normal child in most respects. We took him places with us and tried to live as if nothing in our family was different. Still, there were those times when I sat alone and cried bitterly about our darling little boy. My husband was a great source of strength and comfort to me, but he too had times of despondency and disappointment over having a retarded son. When one was despondent, the other would try to be strong.

We wondered what to do. Year after year we kept hoping that someone would come up with a new idea about why David was the way he was and would produce a miraculous cure. When it did not come, we began to believe that there must be some reason for David's being different.

In situations such as this we must realize that we cannot adjust to so large a problem overnight. Cicero once said, "There is no grief which time does not lessen," and I see that this is true. Many times, however, I wondered why it did not get any easier to bear, and I felt that our prayers were not answered. David had been given a special blessing by Harold B. Lee, one of the general authorities of our church, and I felt that if David was meant to improve, it would surely come after this blessing. As time went on and there was no change, however, we began telling ourselves it was something which was meant to be, and we would just have to accept it.

Gradually we became accustomed to being the parents of a "handicapped child." We decided that we must do everything we could to help David reach whatever potential he had and then try to make the best of whatever came to us. The doctor told us, "Don't expect anything, and then everything you get will be gravy."

David learned to talk enough to make most of his needs known, but sometimes it was very frustrating when he could not make us understand. His speech was very limited but he could say important phrases, like "love you." He seemed to understand what we said to him, but could not always respond. He could learn only certain things and then no more.

No child was loved more than David—by his parents, his loving grandparents and relatives, and our many friends and neighbors. I believe that we all thought we could love David into being normal. If that had been possible, that is what would have taken place, but it did not happen. Nevertheless, we did not ever stop loving him and he always seemed to love us.

Should We See Other Doctors?

When David was four years old he had still not learned to walk by himself. We had taken him to an orthopedic surgeon and everything possible was checked to try and find out if there was any physical reason he couldn't walk. The doctor diagnosed him as having cerebral palsy, along with the mental retardation, and suggested that we have David fitted with full leg braces. He also recommended physical therapy. His body looked normal and healthy, but the soft connective tissues were causing his feet to turn inward and it was hoped that the braces might slow down this process and give him enough support to enable him to walk. His balance was very poor. Many times he would fall backward and bump his head because he was unable to catch himself.

We began taking him to the hospital for therapy to try and strengthen his back and legs. The muscles were becoming very tight and he could not sit on the floor with his legs straight out in front of him. There was a young man at the hospital, Bryan McKendrick, who was a great help to David. He had a kind manner about him, and worked very patiently as David's therapist. He taught me to do the exercises so that we would not have to go to the hospital every day.

I did the exercises with David every day for many months. It did not change the fact that he was not developing normally, but it did improve the strength in his muscles and the time was well spent. He wore his braces day and night and was able to walk alone when he was four-and-a-half years old, although he was still very unstable.

We had no idea what to expect in the future. I think this is the hardest part of having a handicapped child. It was not the things I had to do for David which were a burden to me, but it was the constant problem of trying to control my emotions. Now that I have had the experience of raising a handicapped child, however, I would say to other parents: do not be too sorrowful that your child does not meet all the requirements for what we call "normal," for sometimes it is in the defect that we find the prize. I am fully convinced of that now, though I did not realize at the time what a choice experience we were privileged to have.

We wanted to keep trying to find out why David was the way he was, so we took him to the University of California Medical Center in San Francisco. He was examined by a team of specialists in seven different fields of medicine, including the head of the cerebral palsy diagnostic center. We were hoping to come away with some impressive answer and instructions for treatment, but when the final diagnosis was made, it was the same as before. They did not know the cause of David's problem and there was no treatment.

I knew then that God did not intend that David should be normal, and that we must fully accept the challenge He had given to us, meeting our responsibility the best way we could. Richard L. Evans once said that the greatest blessing that can come after a great sorrow is reconciliation. Without it there is no peace. After a time, we finally experienced that reconciliation.

When our third son was three months old, we moved to a new neighborhood and wondered what the reaction might be. We found people to be very kind and understanding. I think it was because we brought David's problem out into the open. We taught our children that David was their loving brother and we were not ashamed of him because he was different. Those words—mentally retarded—which seemed so terrible at first, soon became a part of our vocabulary and we did not hesitate to use them when necessary.

Can My Child Attend School?

When David was five years old, we felt that he needed the advantage of whatever schooling was available. We knew he could not compete in a normal school situation, but we had heard of the Utah Valley Care and Training Center. (There are more of these schools now than there was then, and education for the retarded is coming more and more into focus.)

It was very difficult to take David to the school and leave him, because he was still a baby in many ways and could not do anything for himself. I soon realized, however, that it was good for both David and for me, and I was very happy for him to have the opportunity to attend the center for a few hours each day.

Their facilities were quite limited at first, but the people who worked there were very kind, and were interested in the welfare and development of each child. We all worked together as parents and people in the community to plan and raise money for a new and larger school. I learned what it was to become sincerely interested in the progress of these children. Some call them the "less fortunate," but in what way are they less fortunate? We, the so-called normal ones are constantly striving to meet the demands of life and to develop our character to the point where we are considered respectable and worth-while human beings. Retarded people seem to already have that inborn trait of happiness and a love for everyone. I believe that their purpose for being the way they are is to teach us patience and understanding, and to give us a chance to serve others in a way which we might not do otherwise. Those of us who have become involved in this service, whether by choice or by chance, have had an advantage over those who have not.

When one has a handicapped child, it is good to become involved with others who have similar problems. I became acquainted with several people who had children attending the care center with David, who were a great help to me. One of them was Myra, with whom we shared a car pool. I was impressed with the patient way she took care of her retarded daughter and the sweet way in which she met her responsibilities. She now cares for an invalid husband, also, and works with the young people in the Church. She has truly learned what service is, and seeing her in action has given me more courage in my life.

As the years passed David did not grow much mentally, but he was becoming physically larger and our problems with him were increasing. He began to create a lot of disturbance in public and it became necessary to leave him at home more of the time. We would either take turns staying home with him or get a sitter. Many times his grandparents helped take care of him. We were very blessed in this way. My parents have made many sacrifices for me, and I often wonder if I can ever measure up to the kind of parents they are. I owe them a debt of gratitude which I can never repay. I have learned that being a parent is one of the greatest tests and challenges that God has given us, and that it is not easy to be strong, patient and kind, even though your heart may be very full of love.

Our fourth son was a beautiful dark-haired child, but had many problems as a baby. He was very cross for the first few years of his life, and David had a difficult time coping with the confusion. Sixteen months later, our fifth son was born. He was a sweet, pleasant child, but developed a stomach problem which required surgery when he was three weeks old. It seemed that our trials grew daily. David wanted so much to tend the babies. It became a constant concern to us. He was not much more than a baby himself in his thinking, but his body was large and fairly strong. He would pick the babies up and carry them like a rag doll. He constantly tried to take them out of the crib or pull them off the couch. I was often beside myself with frustration, fearing that the babies would be injured.

After a time, we began to wonder if we would be able to always keep David home with us. We still loved him as much as ever, and thoughts of not having him with us were the source of much sorrow.

Should We Consider an Institution?

By the time David was twelve years old he was still not completely toilet trained. We had worked with him continually, but we could not depend on him to take care of his own needs all the time. This meant that I had three babies to change and dress. I spent many hours working with David, reading books to him, trying to teach him names of things and colors, but I was not educated in the field of "special" children and could only do what I thought best. He could repeat a few things and did make a little progress, but only to a certain point. He could not seem to remember things from day to day. With two other small children, my time was more and more limited with David. My husband was a great help to me when he was home, but many times he came home from work and found me in tears because of the situation that was developing with David.

We wanted to have a good home life for our children and we wanted David to be a part of it, but we did not want to destroy the closeness which we had with our normal children. David's de- mands were ever-increasing, and as he approached the teen years, his personality was changing somewhat.

Difficult as it was, we decided to visit the Utah State Training School for the retarded. It was a very painful experience for us, and after leaving the school, both my husband and I could not bring ourselves to believe that this was the place for our David. We could not submit the application necessary for his admit- tance. "It can never be," we both agreed. Our dear, sweet, lovable David did not belong there with "those kind" of children. We went home feeling the weight of our responsibility very heavily, and felt very much alone. We wondered what we could ever do about our situation and prayed for guidance and an answer to our problem. We realized that no one else could tell us what to do. The only way to decide such a matter is to weigh all the facts, investigate all the possibilities and then make the decision our- selves—the parents of the child.

We tried employment services and welfare offices for someone to help care for David, but there was no one. We visited foster homes and nursing homes, but found only one which seemed to suit our needs. We tried this for awhile, but it, too, had to be discontinued. After a time, we decided we must visit the Training School again.

The first experience of seeing such an institution can be de- pressing. Some of the chidren are not pleasant to look at, some are not well, and sometimes it does not appear to be a happy place. I want to explain this in detail because I know that there are many parents who are faced with the same decision we had to make. After investigating the school more thoroughly, we came to believe that perhaps they had something to offer our son which we could not provide at home. We could see that he would have good care and would not have to be subjected to the confusion of a busy family life where he must compete with normal children. Still, we were apprehensive about placing David with people who did not love him as we did, and he was such a good looking, healthy boy that he did not seem to fit in with those who were there. We learned, however, that one can look beyond these out- ward, visible appearances and realize that deep inside is a special kind of soul. Then it is possible not only to tolerate them but to love them.

David seemed to have reached his plateau of learning. We could only try not to grieve over his condition, but to go on loving him and seeing that he had the best possible care. Our religious beliefs taught us that he did not need to advance in this life, but only to come to this earth to receive a mortal body. This gave us a great deal of encouragement and hope, our knowing that this was not all there was for David. Someday he would progress and have all that anyone else would ever have. These beliefs became the backbone of our understanding and the only way by which we could fully accept and make the best of David's problem. Having these teachings to believe in made it easier to cope with and work out the disappointments which we often felt.

At the Training School we were shown around the campus and became better acquainted with the many programs available. We learned that there are many opportunities for the retarded which we could not get anywhere else. We realized that our first impressions of institution life were somewhat drastic, and we must look at it with our hearts, not only our eyes. We talked to friends who had children there, and it helped to know that they were pleased with the care. We found that the Training School was not a place full of children who were unwanted, but many who were deeply loved and missed by their families. We learned that David would be able to attend school for whatever learning he was able to accomplish, that he would be given recreation and therapy activities, could attend church, and would be taken to many parks, parades, and the canyon. There would be good medical care—doctors, dentists and medication available when needed, as well as a hospital if necessary. For the first time in David's life, we felt that perhaps living at home was not the best place for him, that maybe he would actually gain more from being at the school, living with others like him. And they *were* like him, in many ways, as much as we hated to admit it.

David's abilities were not improving. He seemed unable to cope with his growing body and his feet were becoming more and more crippled. Surgery was tried but was not the answer to his crippling condition. My own health problems were growing worse, and there were times when I had so little strength that I could hardly keep up with all I had to do. I had spent some time in the hospital, and it was upon my doctor's advice that we decided to submit an application to the Training School for David's admittance. We did not expect it to come so soon, as we had been told there was a long waiting list. After the necessary shots, examinations and preparations, we took him to the school and said our temporary goodbyes. He cried and we cried, too, and it was like tearing off an arm when we had to drive away and leave him. We had dreaded this moment all his life, but knew we had to face it the best way we could. We knew that being away from David would not make us love him any less, and we felt that it was the best thing for everyone involved.

David was twelve years old when we took him to the school, but his mind was still that of a baby. I wanted to go to him every day, but we had been asked not to come back for two weeks, to help with his adjustment. It seemed unfair, and I'm sure he thought we had abandoned him, but after many sleepless nights and guilty feelings, we all became adjusted to it. He was placed in a nice building where he could be taught whatever habits he was capable of establishing. Much individual help was given to him and the people who worked with him were concerned and kind. Activities were well supervised, and we felt good about the way things were, even though I cannot say we were "happy" about it. It broke our hearts every time we drove away and left him watching us from the window, but we never left without telling him we loved him and that we would be back. We brought him home often for visits and holidays, and though it was a situation which gave us much relief from the constant care of the twelve years we had had him, we never became completely reconciled to his being away from home.

In our family we always prayed for David—mostly that he would be well taken care of and that he would be happy and know that we still loved him. Some days we still had problems when he was home, but most of the time he brought a kind of love and joy into the family which we did not feel when he was gone. He always came into the house with a smile and a happy look on his face, and would say, "Hi, Mama," as soon as he saw me. He showed his love for all people—for those who worked with him, for all family and relatives and even for people he did not know. There was something about David, people said, a kind of radiance that was very special. People at the Training School have often told us how much they loved him and how he brought joy to everyone. He had a sense of humor which is not always evident with children as retarded as he was.

We wanted so much to be able to help our son. Whenever he had a medical problem, it was immediately taken care of. His teeth were kept in good condition, and we encouraged proper skin care. We appreciated all that was done for him, and did not want him to ever be neglected in any way. It takes special people to work with the retarded, and I have a great admiration for them. Those who successfully do it are people who really care about others and have a deep love for these children. We received calls from some of the foster mothers who said, "You don't need to worry about David when I am taking care of him. I love him as though he were my own and it is a joy to be with him." This was a great comfort to me and I will always be grateful to those "mothers" who cared for him and showed him the love he needed when I could not be with him.

There are many details which could be told about David's life and his stay at the Training School, but the most important thing about his story is that he had a profound effect on all those who knew him well. At eighteen years of age, there was not much that he could do, but he became noticeably changed—he was easily managed, caused very little disturbance and seemed even more loving than before. My feelings were again filled with emotion. If he had been normal, he would now be graduating from high school and perhaps preparing for a missionary assignment for the church. Seeing other boys doing these things at this age made us more aware of the disappointments we had earlier felt upon learning that David had a definite abnormality. It seemed so long ago and yet like yesterday. I felt a sense of loss that David would never do these things, yet I was also grateful, in a way, that he would never have to face the problems and trials of the world. I became more and more convinced that David was the one who was blessed. We, too, had been blessed in many ways. Over the seven years he had been at the Training School our love and concern for him had not diminished in any way, but had continued to grow and become even more important to our family. David always returned that love abundantly. Even when he was not able to cope with certain problems, he would soon become sweet and lovable again. Whenever he was home we all tried to be at our best. We came to realize that if there were no other reason for his existence in this life, we will always remember that where he was, there was love.

We knew that David's physical condition would grow progressively worse and that his mental condition would never improve. We talked about it often, and I often had the feeling that perhaps he would not be with us much longer in this life. As he reached the age of nineteen, I had the strong feeling that there was going to be a change in his life. I thought perhaps the Lord would call him to fulfill the mission I had always wanted him to have. I knew it could never be in this world, and so I wondered.

On October fifteenth, 1975, our family was all at home when a call came from the Training School, telling us that David had suddenly become critically ill and had been taken in an ambulance to a Salt Lake City hospital. He had been perfectly well that day and they did not seem to know the nature of his illness. When I called the hospital, they told me that he had passed away on the way to Salt Lake. It was unbelievable! How could it happen so fast? So many things flashed through my mind! We had faced many difficult times in David's life, but this came so unexpectedly and without warning. It was as if his time on earth simply came to an end.

After the initial shock of his passing, I began to realize how much we had been blessed and how my teachings had helped me get through the past nineteen years. I fully believe that there was a purpose for David's life here, and that was to teach us the true meaning of love and better understanding. I believe that David is now busily engaged in teaching others that great kind of love he had, fulfilling the mission he could not do here. Free of his own limitations of body and mind, he can now find satisfaction in doing the great work of the Lord, that of teaching the gospel of love, the love for which he had such a great capacity.

My love for David was, and is, deeper than I can ever say, and because of this I have shed many tears—not tears of sorrow or regret, but of loneliness and the desire to be with him. I know that I must not grieve, for David is surely blessed much more than I. He was truly a source of joy in this life, even though we had many trials in raising him. We feel that his spirit was so sweet and special that it greatly overshadowed the sorrow and unhappiness of his handicap. The problems were brought about because of the weaknesses of the flesh in this mortal existence, but they have now all become insignificant and almost forgotten in comparison to the lessons they taught us. We will greatly miss the sweet spirit which radiated from David, and if we grieve, it shall be for ourselves that we must go on without him in the struggle for a righteous existence. But we rejoice in the knowledge that he has gone to a better life than he had here, even with all the love that we gave him. And what could be better than the love that we gave him? Only the glorious and eternal love of God.

*   *   *

"We cannot always understand the plan of the Almighty—the thing that seems like a disaster is often a blessing in disguise."

—Melvin J. Ballard

NO SAD GOODBYES

No sad goodbyes,
I told myself;
He left this world so pure
  and undefiled.
What one of us can be so sure
Of going back to God
As clean as when we came?
And who has brought more love
  than he has brought?
Yet, when he left,
My heart was heavy as a stone,
Not in despair, nor lack of faith,
  and not without
Much comfort from above
Did I exist and face each day;
But never have I felt such loneliness:
Each morning when I wake,
  I think of him,
And every night,
And all the in-betweens.
They tell me it will lessen,
  that, in time, the pain will go,
  and so
I try to fill my mind
With thoughts of him there
Where relatives will greet him
With rejoicing and with love
  Far greater
  than the tears which we have shed
When we said
Our sad goodbyes.

—Sherrie A. Hundley

*K*eith J. Karren was born in England and raised in Southern Alberta, Canada. His wife, the former Diane Johnson, was born and raised in Grantsville, Utah. They met while both were serving an LDS mission to Great Britain. A BYU romance set the stage for their marriage.

Through the years since their marriage in 1967, education pursuits and teaching led the Karrens to Ricks College in Rexburg, Idaho, and Oregon State University where Keith received his Ph.D. in Health Sciences. It was in Corvallis, Oregon that a very difficult maternal labor finally produced a little boy that was destined for a problem start in life.

The Karrens feel that life is a great university and that education is a lifelong matter. Some periods of life are more educating than others. The story of the Karren's son, Jamie Todd, is an example of just that. Keith and Diane feel that testimonies of the Gospel of Jesus Christ have been made even stronger with experiences such as this. The Karrens now live in Provo, Utah, with their four children. Keith currently teaches in the Department of Health Sciences at Brigham Young University.

Chapter 2

Our Long Wait

Story of Jamie Todd Karren

"Faith is to believe what we do not see; and the reward of faith is to see what we believe." —St. Augustine

In June, 1974, my family was located at Oregon State University in Corvallis, Oregon. I was on sabbatical leave from BYU and busily pursuing a Ph.D. in Health Science. My wife, Diane, had previously developed a disease called endometriosis and her opportunity to have more children was threatened. So it was with excited enthusiasm that we had greeted the news of her pregnancy in November 1973.

The day of delivery approached rapidly and the vibrant Oregon June scenery and weather set the stage for this blessing to enter our family. Then he came, and his trip from the protecting and peaceful womb to the noise, bright lights, and cooling air was difficult and long. Diane had struggled through the night, and though she had worked hard and courageously, the labor was termed inefficient. Finally, a quick-thinking obstetrician used forceps to guide the large baby head into a workable position and the umbilical cord which sustained the baby's life was twice unwrapped from the baby's neck. That was how he entered the world, and Diane and I had the great blessing for which we had prayed long and hard. Jamie Todd, our third born,

33

was as loved by parents, brother and sister, as any child could be.

Soon we were back home in Utah. We had noticed no startling problems with Jamie Todd's growth and development. It was true that his head seemed extra large and his tiny legs were so skinny and still, but we told ourselves that he was so responsive and happy; he would catch up.

In January 1975, I was facilitating a mental health discussion in a personal health class. A department secretary notified me that my wife was waiting outside the Richards Building in the car and it was extremely important that I come right down. I turned the class over to a Graduate Assistant and scurried outside. The scene that greeted me caused an immediate ache in my heart and puzzlement in my brain. Diane was clutching a sobbing Jamie Todd, her own face twisted in agonized crying. I slid in beside her and slowly, between sobs, the horrifying news stumbled out. Diane had just taken our little seven-month old to the pediatrician for his check-up. The doctor had slowly felt, tested, measured, and observed. Finally he explained that he had been carefully watching Jamie Todd for weeks and his suspicions were finally confirmed; Jamie Todd had a form of cerebral palsy that affected muscle coordination in the legs. The muscles weren't receiving messages from the brain and they were not growing. Jamie Todd may never be able to walk!

I will never forget the long ride home to Springville that cold January afternoon. It seemed as though one side of my brain was numbly occupied with thoughts of this tragic news and the other side busily trying to supply support to Diane whose heart was sick and full of disbelief. At home we sat for a long time and held each other and little Jamie Todd tight. His trusting, innocent eyes showed bewilderment at this strange experience he was having. We talked about what would become of him, how would other kids treat him as he grew up, would he ever be a father and have children of his own? Maybe I could rig up a special saddle so he could ride our horse! We were seized with an urgency to contact the Pediatric Neurology specialist to whom our pediatrician had referred us. We wanted to see him now, tomorrow, but the receptionist firmly explained that the first opening was the following week.

What a long week! We were so anxious to get there, and yet held back in dread. We found ourselves carefully watching every move Jamie Todd made that week, looking for any physical sign to show movement in his legs and telling each other how mentally alert he was! We found ourselves unusually sensitive to each other's needs and seemed to spend more time with the other two children. A part of that long week was spent in earnestly seeking for spiritual help. Diane and I are both active in the Latter-day Saint faith. We believe strongly in the power of prayer, fasting, and laying on of hands by priesthood holders. We prepared ourselves and on the following Sunday my Father-in-law, President Kenneth C. Johnson of Grantsville, Utah, and I blessed little Jamie Todd. It was a powerful experience. The spirit was strong, the words flowed, and I spiritually felt the healing blessing I had given would come to pass.

Then came the visit to the Neurological Specialist at the University Medical Center in Salt Lake City. In the waiting room we found ourselves surrounded by other parents whose children may or did have neurological problems. At first everyone was silent and held their child protectively, but soon the kids were on the floor playing and the parents slowly began to share feelings— "Our little boy has seizures but we hope medications will control it." "Gosh, he is such a cute little thing. Our little girl had oxygen deprivation when she was being born. We hope nothing is too seriously wrong." "Oh, I'm sure she will be okay. Our little guy isn't developing in his legs like he should." (For some reason I held back on the words—cerebral palsy.)

It was finally our turn. Two doctors took Jamie Todd to a testing office and were there for hours, it seemed. We secretly hoped with all our heart that they would walk in with big smiles on their faces and announce, "This little boy is completely normal!" But they didn't.

The diagnosis confirmed our pediatrician's suspicions that the muscles in the legs and buttocks were not developing. Jamie Todd also manifested other signs that suggested a type of cerebral palsy. "But he is so young and we can't be sure. It is not an extremely serious case if he does have C.P. Mentally he is very bright." Those words from the head Pediatric Neurologist lifted us considerably.

Shortly after, we excitedly observed Jamie Todd becoming more physically active, turning over, and beginning to move those skinny little legs. The movement got better and better. Each night we would tell each other we just knew his legs were getting bigger. Our pediatrician wasn't nearly so sure, but Jamie's head was growing normally and now not so macrocephalic (big head) as at birth. More visits were made to Salt Lake City and finally, at thirteen months, Jamie Todd was declared completely normal!

Every so often Diane and I talk about our experience with cerebral palsy. Certainly we are elated that Jamie Todd doesn't have it. We look upon it as a great spiritual blessing. Could we have handled the situation had it turned out differently? Yes, I think so. Why was Jamie Todd blessed but so many other children go through life with cerebral palsy? Could it be that a handicap could turn out to bring great blessings to a family and the individual involved, even reaching into the next life? We have decided that attitude is the key, and have grown in many ways as the story of this little boy's life continues to unfold.

Jim Christensen was a healthy, normal boy until the age of fourteen when his life was suddenly and tragically reshaped by a truck-train collision near his home in Moroni, Utah. Doctors said he would be nothing but a vegetable—a useless, incurable case confined to a special home for the rest of his life. Yet in a few years Jim was capable of doing things that people said he could never do.

Had he not been blessed with parents who loved him and whose faith would not allow him to give up, Jim would not have been able to overcome the unsurmountable obstacles which faced him, and would have spent his life as a useless cripple.

Jim later died while serving a mission for his church in the Kentucky-Louisville missionfield. There again he was called upon to face trials, and his courage was greatly tested. But for many years after his train accident, he proved that he could live a useful life, and exhibited an endless desire to make the best of his problems.

Gwen and Eslie Christensen, his parents, have lived all their lives in a small country town, raising a large family and operating a successful turkey business. There they have invested their time, their love and their devotion to those things which are meaningful in life, finding gratification in strong family ties, church responsibilities and hard work. Theirs has not been an easy life, but they know, as many do, that it is only in the diligent pursuance of challenging experiences that we really find growth, satisfaction and everlasting joy.

S.A.H.

Chapter 3

"Doctor, Where Is Your Faith"

Story of Jim Christensen

"Impossible is a word only to be found in the dictionary of fools."
　　　　　　　　　　　　　　　—Napoleon Bonaparte

Jim was a normal, average, small-town boy—good natured, religious, the oldest of seven children. He played baseball, took piano lessons and worked with his father on their large turkey ranch. He loved to fish and hunt, and by the time he was fourteen, he could down a rabbit on the dead run with his twenty-two. But before Jim had turned fifteen, these things all came to an abrupt end.

Jim's story is one of love, dedication, hard work and faith. Some may say that it is a story of tragedy and did not end happily. Yet knowing of the great accomplishments which he achieved and the kind of life that he lived, we can see that his time on earth was neither wasted nor unimportant. And if we believe at all in the concept of a life after this one and that our station there depends upon what we have done here, then we know that Jim has found the happiness he deserved. In the twenty-four years that he spent on this earth and especially during the last ten, Jim gave something special to the world and those close to him—the example of complete dedication to meeting life's trials bravely and accomplishing what he set out to do.

Two weeks before Christmas in 1966, a grief-stricken mother drove over a hundred miles almost daily to a Salt Lake City hospital to visit her injured son. It meant spending a lot of time on the road, leaving six other children at home. It meant many sleepless hours at the hospital—anxious, wondering hours—but she wanted to be there when Jim regained consciousness. Her husband was spending all but a few hours a night at the hospital—watching for some sign that Jim would be all right. They had had such hopes for their oldest son—college, a mission, marriage. Perhaps he would take over his father's business.

Jim was an active, eager young man. He and his cousin, Boyd, had talked of going for Christmas trees ever since Thanksgiving Day. On December 10, Boyd picked Jim up, eager and ready for the trip. They took some sandwiches and hot chocolate and anxiously headed the pickup truck toward Fairview Canyon. It was a sunny day, but cold, and they were glad they had dressed warmly. Jim loved the out-doors, had hunted in these mountains often near his home, and enjoyed the smell of the clean, quiet air. Nothing was finer in the world, as far as Jim was concerned, than to get out into the mountains. As a small child he had gone with his father often to hunt or just to ride, and although sometimes it was bitter cold, his strong determination had kept him going when many boys would have given up.

Jim and Boyd drove up the canyon as far as they could, pulled off the road and went down the side of the mountain to cut trees. When they had cut enough, they dragged them back and loaded them onto the truck and headed down the canyon toward home. It had been a wonderful day! The snow was sparkling beautifully in the sun, and the crisp air made them tingle. It was just the kind of day that made one glad to be alive.

Between Mt. Pleasant and Fairview, a train inched its way along through the fields. Jim noticed the train, but didn't pay much attention, as he was still feeling the glow of having spent such a great day in the mountains. He and Boyd talked of different things, enjoying the ride.

Suddenly, a train whistle blew—loud and shrill and dreadful! And then Jim remembered nothing.

A few minutes later, a young mother drove toward Mt. Pleasant and saw that there had been an accident. She soon learned that the train had collided with her husband, Boyd's, truck—a pickup full of Christmas trees.

When the truck had reached the depot which stands close to the tracks, there were no lights flashing, no gates down, nothing. Only the sudden, piercing whistle of the train, as it came roaring at them from behind the depot.

Both boys were thrown from the truck and were badly injured. They were taken to a nearby hospital, where it was learned that Jim's condition was very serious. He was transferred to Salt Lake City, where his mother and father waited day and night for him to regain consciousness.

One of the legs was badly hurt, but the most serious of his injuries was a depressed skull fracture and a large cut on the left side of his head. Such an injury can and did destroy many brain cells, causing unconsciousness and a severe palsy condition on Jim's right side.

The sight was not pleasant as he lay helpless in the intensive care unit with tubes in his nose and arms. Because of the severe injury and shock to his brain, his temperature rose sharply and remained high. He was kept on an ice mattress to try and lower the temperature of his body and to keep the swelling of the brain down. For three weeks this procedure was used. It helped in keeping the temperature controlled, but he developed pneumonia. A tracheotomy had to be performed so that the mucous could be extracted from his lungs, and he was given high doses of penicillin.

Still, Jim did not regain consciousness. His injured brain could not respond to his body needs, and his arms and legs flailed uncontrollably, until the skin was rubbed almost off. His parents sat beside his bed day after day, doing whatever they could to help—watching, hoping, praying. His father stayed in Salt Lake all the time and his mother drove the many miles back and forth to see her son, not well herself from problems of her last baby's birth only six weeks before. The doctors gave them no hope for Jim's recovery. It was only through many days of fasting and prayer that they were able to keep up their courage and find strength to face their dilemma.

Jim was given a special blessing. When Elder Harold B. Lee had finished, he shook the hands of each member of the family and said, "Whatever you do, don't give up your faith. Your son can be well again."

Jim's parents never doubted that Jim would live, though they must have realized that it would probably be a long, hard pull—a trial which they must not only witness, but in which they would play a very large part. Their faith was strong, for they lived by the

words of Him who has said, "In the world ye shall have tribulation. But be of good cheer; I have overcome the world." (John
16:33)

Sometimes it is very difficult to separate our wants and
desires from the things that are for our best good. Sometimes we
wonder whether or not we should ask for the life of a loved one to
be spared. Jim's parents had confidence that the Lord would
direct whatever happened, and they put the entire matter into His
hands, knowing that He alone would know what was best for Jim.

Christmas was not far off, but the hope of a joyful one was
very bleak. Friends and relatives took care of the family and the
home while the parents were away. Christmas preparations went
on as usual for the other children, and Gwen and Eslie
Christensen found that this was one of those times when friends
were really appreciated.

Christmas came and went, but Jim was still unconscious.
For two months he lay in a state of unpredictable semi-life,
slowly wasting away, with no one knowing what the outcome
would be or what to do for him. His mother and father continued
to help him in any way they could, and no one will ever really
know what feelings of sorrow and frustration they felt, what tiring
efforts they made, or how many hours of sleep they lost.

Gradually, Jim began to show signs of awareness. At times
he was able to open his eyes and the doctors and nurses would
talk to him and try to get a response, but without success. It
seemed that he could hear them, but did not have the ability to
respond. He was like a newborn baby, unable to control his
movements, his voice or even his thoughts.

The doctor spoke to Jim's mother. "Have you made up your
mind what to do about this boy?" he asked.

"What do you mean?" she replied.

"It's time," the doctor said, "that you accepted the fact that
your son will never again be normal. You must find a nursing
home someplace for him and try to make the best of it. Jim will
never be anything but a vegetable."

She hesitated for a moment and then said, "Doctor, *where* is
your faith?"

The doctor looked grave. "There's a difference between faith
and reality," he said, "and the reality of this case is that the boy
will never recover."

Gwen and Eslie Christensen still did not give up. They were
determined that they would not send him to a nursing home. "We
stayed by his side and saw to his every need," explained his

mother, "and there is no doubt in our minds that it was only through this constant watchfulness and deep concern for him that he began to make some improvement. They later commented:

"We arranged for him to be fed some solid foods. They had to be osterized and put directly into his stomach through a tube in his nose, but we insisted that it was done, and before long Jim began to show signs of change."

The doctors continually tried to get him to show that he could understand. They told him to stick out his tongue or make some sign, but with no success. The nurses tried, too, but Jim did not respond. It was only after many, many tries by his father that he finally stuck out his tongue to show that he understood.

"That was a great moment for me," said his father, "but I knew there was still a long way to go. I wondered what was to be, and decided to make it a matter of special prayer. I asked whether or not our son would ever speak again. The answer came in the form of a dream, in which Jim appeared, looking completely well and recovered. He stood there looking at me, and then said, 'Hi, Dad,' two simple, but meaningful words. Then I knew that some-day Jim would speak to us again. We were both sure of it. It would be a test and a trial for us, but together we would work it out."

Jim was released from the hospital, with no instructions whatsoever for his care. They were well aware, however, of the special and constant attention he would need. It was difficult knowing just where to begin in the long journey of getting Jim back to the point where he was really living again. They had brought him this far, and they would not give up now.

Jim could not be taken home just yet. He was admitted to the hospital close to his home, where his father and mother went every day to help with his care. Although he could not speak to them, he seemed to understand. Repeatedly, they said to him, "We love you, son. You're going to be okay." Or, "Don't worry, Jim, you're going to get well."

On Valentine's Day, the other children of the family made valentines and took them to the hospital. He seemed to know them all and was happy to see them. Before the visit was over, Jim rewarded them all by speaking their names—for the first time since the accident.

Things seemed to be looking better all the time, but it was evident that Jim was having to learn everything all over again, just as a little child would do. His family was willing and anxious to help him. They are a family who love each other, who care

about each other's welfare. They were determined to do everything in their power to help Jim recover what he had lost. At
times the discouragement was overwhelming, life was seemingly
difficult and unfair. The days were sometimes long and the
nights sleepless. Yet they did not give in to those feelings of
despair.

About a week after the change in hospitals, it was decided
that Jim could be taken home. From a hospital bed in his room,
he again became part of the family that he loved and wanted to be
near.

Progress was slow, but it did come. Hours of personal care,
helping, teaching and training stretched into months. Together
they all began to fit the pieces of Jim's shattered life together
again, to help him regain those things which had been part of his
fourteen years of life, but suddenly lost in some cavern of forget-
fulness.

His father took care of his personal needs, taught him to
walk again and gave him the continuing love, strength and hope
that he needed. Jim had to be told over and over again what had
happened to him, and to be reassured that Boyd was not still
back on the tracks.

Jim told me that whenever he felt frightened or discouraged,
it was his mother and father who brought him out of it by telling
him to make the most of what he had. Even in the worst of conditions, there is always something to be grateful for, no matter
how small, and no matter how large the problems may appear. To
some, a problem may be greater than to others, and we may find
it harder to live with than the other fellow. It mainly depends on
our attitude and our desire to make the most of life. A great educator once said that where one man finds an obstacle a stumbling
block, another finds it a stepping stone.

When Jim really became aware of his problems and of what
his future might be, he determined not to give up. Something
made him want to go on and keep trying, to climb out of this deep
pit of helplessness and make it on his own. His body and mind
were injured and weak, but not his spirit nor his determination.
He felt that what had happened to him was just part of life, and
he would have to make the best of it.

In spite of his courageous outlook, however, there were
countless times when the problem seemed too difficult. He often
felt cheated at not being able to do what other kids his age could
do. One of his biggest problems was that his status in the family
had changed. He had always been the big brother, the leader, the

one to shoulder some of the family responsibility. Now his physical disabilities made this impossible.

"It was difficult for me to have to step down," Jim related. "I felt a resentment which I had to fight to overcome, but I always had hope that someday I would be all right and that in due time I would gain control of my reflexes."

He still loved the out-doors. His father would take him when he went to work with the turkeys, even though Jim could only lie helplessly and watch his father. Yet he said to himself often, "Someday...someday I'll be able to help again."

When fall came his father took him hunting with the family, even though he still had many problems and could not carry a gun. He enjoyed being with his family, and it helped him to know that he was still considered one of the family.

Friends came to see him often. When he was able to go with them, they would often take him to the activities around town. He could not go back to school the rest of that year, but wanted to finish high school. His parents arranged for a tutor to come to their home and work with him. He was also taken back to Salt Lake many times, where he was under a rehabilitation program.

When he did go back to school, it was a strenuous and trying experience. Getting to classes took extra time, and someone else had to carry his books. He could still not walk very well. When he had first tried, his injured leg was still badly bruised and sore, and caused him much pain. He had used a wheelchair for some time, then walked with a walker, and now was using two canes. Progress was slow and sometimes torturous. It required a great deal of practice, hard work and patience.

At school Jim found everyone understanding and helpful. Both teachers and students did whatever they could to help, and though he was not at the top of his class as he had been before, he was not at the bottom. The other students seemed concerned about his progress and treated him very well. This fact seemed to be the thing that kept Jim going and from becoming too discouraged. The real show of love, the tremendous outpouring of compassion was what gave him the courage to try harder. He wanted to show everyone that he could do it.

This kind of determination moved Jim toward the completion of high school—quite an accomplishment for someone who had been declared a vegetable. While in high school he was a member of the chorus; the Future Farmers of America, where he won several awards for his turkey growing; he graduated from four years of L.D.S. Seminary, and passed his hunter's safety course with a score of 100%, even though control of his reflexes was still somewhat impaired.

One of Jim's special dreams has always been to fulfill a mission for the Church. His family wondered how this could now be possible, for though he had made tremendous accomplishments, he was still not completely independent. He walked unsteadily, he had never regained the full use of one of his hands, and tying shoes, preparing food, etc., was difficult. He had worked very hard to be able to learn everything all over again and was fairly capable at taking care of himself, but there were things with which he would still need help. No matter how hard he tried, he was not quite the same and could not do all he wanted to do. He had been driving the tractor for his dad, could plow around eighty acres alone, but there had been accidents, too, and it was a great concern to his parents.

Jim tried college, but felt that he was not suited to it. He went to work with his father, as he had said he would someday do. He later worked at the turkey processing plant near his home, but was never satisfied with what he was doing because he wanted to better himself. His strong love of life was not destroyed in the accident nor was his strong will, and they grew with his continued efforts.

Yet in his heart, he knew there were some things he must accept. He would probably never be physically able to do all the things he could do before. The only thing to do was to try and enjoy every moment of life that he could, to the fullest of his ability, and to be grateful for all that God had returned to him.

Most of the time Jim was well and happy. He still had a physical handicap, but his friendly, pleasant personality was there and his sweet spirit was not affected, unless to make him even more aware of the joy of living and the mercy of God's great blessings to him.

When things got to the point that Jim wanted to strike out on his own, his parents helped him to find something which would give him the opportunity for more spiritual growth. They did not know whether he would ever be able to go on a mission or not. He had proved that he could overcome great obstacles and handicaps. He had taught the muscles of his body to overcome the involuntary spasms, the uncontrolled movements to a large extent. Now he needed something to develop the muscles of his spiritual self. He was well aware that happiness comes to an individual in many forms, and that we find it not only by seeking and taking, but by creating and giving.

individual in many forms, and that we find it not only by seeking and taking, but by creating and giving.

Jim was not sure what he was going to do with his life, but he did want to do something worth-while. He took a job in Provo and was called upon to speak in church meetings, inspiringly telling his listeners of his strong testimony of the gospel of Jesus Christ. He was an excellent example of what faith and hard work can do in overcoming an extremely difficult handicap.

Then came the greatest of Jim's many blessings. He was called to serve in the Kentucky-Louisville mission for the Church, and for twenty-two months was busily and happily engaged in doing the Lord's work, the thing he most wanted to do. After being told of Jim's problems, a woman in the mission field wrote to one of his relatives and said, "I did not even notice he had a handicap. He seemed just like the other missionaries." Another one wrote, "I can't tell you how much his testimony has helped us all. He has been a great example to us, and has especially helped my young son, who also wants to go on a mission."

Jim's parents received many such letters from people who have been touched by his life, letting them know what a great job he was doing, how they loved him, and what a special spirit he had.

Then, suddenly, the Christensens had another tragic shock come into their lives. They received word that Jim had been taken to a hospital, where he died of a cerebral hemorrhage, two months before he was to complete his mission and return home.

Was this the pay for the hours of work, the tears of sorrow, the strain of disappointment which they had endured? Is there any satisfaction now to his parents in knowing that his life was once saved and most of his abilities restored, only to be taken away so suddenly? In spite of the sorrow and hard work which these parents had to bear, I believe there is great satisfaction in what they were able to help Jim accomplish. And, if necessary, I think they would do it again.

The Christensens are grateful for the knowledge that there is a life after this one, and that there is something for us to do there as well as there is here. His mother has said, "We know our dear Jim is busier than ever before and that he wouldn't want us to hold him back. We take comfort in knowing that he is happy."

They also were able to take comfort in the words of Jim's former mission president, George Durrant, when he said at Jim's funeral: "There is not a better missionary in the Kentucky-Louisville mission than Elder Christensen; there never was, and there never will be."

Jim cheerfully met his responsibilities in the best way he could with what he had, and he met his trials bravely. When sorrow and suffering came, he found strength and reassurance in the gospel. "Blessed is he that keepeth my commandments, whether in life or in death; and he that is faithful in tribulation, the reward of the same is greater in the kingdom of heaven." (D & C 58:2.)

William Jordan once wrote that life is a wondrously complex problem, until we come to the realization that it *can* be made simpler. He has said that at times we all wonder why life is as it is and why some people have so many trials and others do not. We must have the faith to know that only God knows the answer, and He will not demand of any of us more than the best we can give.

After Jim's accident with the train he was given a special blessing by a patriarch of the L.D.S. Church, in which many wonderful promises were made to him if he would walk obediently and humbly before the Lord. He was told that there had never been an accident which had had the effect upon the whole community as his had. He was a boy loved by everyone, admired by everyone, and when he was hurt so badly and he lay hovering between life and death, everyone prayed for him—young people, old people and little children—that he might recover. His parents received letters from as far as California from people who expressed their concern. Everyone was impressed by the way Jim made such a remarkable and miraculous comeback. His courage, his faith and his confidence were a great example and inspiration to all.

He was also promised that there was a mission in life for him and that he would fulfill it, that he would go into the mission field and teach the gospel of Jesus Christ. He was encouraged to keep smiling, to keep praying, and to keep plodding onward. This he did, and as he was promised, he was blessed with patience, with wisdom, with hope and fulfillment. He was also promised that some day he would look back and say, "Father, I thank thee for all that has happened to me. I now see why."

There is a saying that goes something like this: Great is the man who kindles a light in the world, but greater is the man who walks through the dark paths of life, himself a light.

Jim was that kind of man.

TO EACH A ROSE, TO EACH A THORN

He had his share of life's vicissitudes;
The stinging pricks, the thorn bush, all were there;
No bed of roses for reflective moods—
Beneath his feet, the spiny prickly pear.

Yet there is beauty in a cactus flower,
And softness to be found in thistle down;
The sweetest perfume in the arbored bower
Will have to be the rose. It is well known.

Where nettled vines are matted, interlaced,
Small nesting birds will sing their mating song;
And blackberries will ripen—sweet to taste—
When we have patience—faith to wait that long.

(Patience is faith; faith patience. Done and said,
All blackberries are green when they are red.)

He found these goodnesses; and what is more,
He learned to share them. What more could we ask?
Which one of us, when tallying the score
Could better it? For all life is a task.

To each and every one who chooses life
Is given all the burden he can heft.
(Sometimes we count the weight, the struggle, strife,
And wonder if The Powers have any left!)

We analyze our pack; all is confessed:
He never gives us more than we can carry.
Item for item—put it to the test.
It is a law; and it will never vary.

God gives to each a rose, to each a thorn.
Which will we carry home that Glorious Morn?

—Ora Pate Stewart

I first met Marilyn Stanley about twenty years ago, even before she was the mother of a handicapped child. She was an elementary school teacher, with a master's degree in education and had done some work in the field of handicapped children. Her husband, Neldon, a junior high school physical education teacher and a mission president in the B.Y.U. Third Stake, has worked with people from all over the world. While on a mission for the Church he was endowed with a special gift of being able to translate for the deaf. Experiences such as these partly prepared the Stanleys for their having a handicapped child of their own, yet who is ever really prepared for this type of experience? Not only was their little Merrill afflicted with some unknown malady which gave him many physical problems, he was also mentally retarded.

Marilyn and Neldon have been able to relate well to many children with problems. Besides raising their own family of nine, they have been foster parents to a young Indian girl as well as to other children. They have learned much from their experiences and feel that the gospel of Jesus Christ is the greatest source of help and support in coping with the problems of having a retarded child, as we are taught that they are indeed special spirits and have a definite purpose in this life, as well as the next.

Marilyn feels that at times her faith and courage were greatly challenged, yet her insight and understanding were increased through the parenting of a child with problems such as Merrill had. She also feels that the sharing of his story may help others to overcome the disappointment and shock of finding that these things can happen to anyone.

S.A.H.

Chapter 4

The Understanding Heart

Story of Merrill Stanley

"God, grant to me the highest art;
Give me the understanding heart."

—Anonymous

Little Merrill's problems did not show up at birth. It was not until a few weeks later, when babies should be gaining some weight, that his parents suspected something might be wrong. Even then, the doctor supposed it was only that Merrill might not be getting enough milk from his mother, and it was suggested that the baby be changed to other diets and food supplements.

This did not prove to be the answer. Merrill seemed to be allergic to whatever supplement was given him. He was unable to tolerate any diet and could keep nothing down. No matter what his mother tried, it did not work and Merrill was becoming weaker and weaker every day. He cried continuously, making it impossible for his mother to get enough sleep. Medications did not even prove helpful and the situation continued to baffle the child's doctors and his parents.

A series of tests were made of the esophagus, the digestive tract, the stomach. None of these revealed any problem. Marilyn and Neldon prayed and searched for an answer. How could this be? Surely there was a reason, but nothing could be found to be causing the problem. Their time and energies were devoted to the continuing struggle of trying to find out why Merrill could not tolerate his food. It was only after putting him back on mother's milk, which was provided by a young mother who lived near the Stanleys, that Merrill began to show a little progress.

Eventually he was able to keep food down. When he was about a year old, he would eat enormous amounts of food, but even this did not appear to be the solution to his problem. He was still not gaining weight normally.

At this point Merrill was taken to the University of Utah and again given extensive tests, but it was never determined why his food did not do him the good he needed. It was keeping him alive, but that was about all. There seemed to be no answer. The doctors could only assume that it was due to some kind of amino acid deficiency and that his protein was not being properly utilized.

In the process of these trying times, many prayers were offered in Merrill's behalf. At first Marilyn had great faith, but in time she began to wonder why their prayers seemingly went unanswered. There came feelings of guilt, of anger, even hatred—not hatred for the child, but hatred toward the situation which they must endure. Why, oh why, must they endure so much? Yet she wondered at her feelings. How could she feel so hateful one day and so loving the next? The anger and frustration always seemed to pass, and then the overwhelming feelings of love for this little curly-headed boy would always return.

Soon Marilyn began to realize that feelings such as these were very normal, under the circumstances. Any parent would feel frustrated, upset, angry, after such an ordeal. It was not so much how she felt about it as how she handled it that mattered. She could see that now. Merrill was her son and he needed her. Oh, how he needed her! She realized how she would have to work to control her feelings so that she might give her best to this child, and also to her young daughter. Through the days of uncertainty she continued to labor. She cared for Merrill and gave him all that a mother can give. But many times she wondered, "Why doesn't he smile for me? Oh, if only he would smile."

Wondering what the future held in store for them was one of the most difficult of the Stanleys' challenges. Could Merrill live with this problem? Could they, as his parents, cope with it? Should they have more children? The doctors had advised them to have no more. Neldon and Marilyn did not want to give up their plans to have more children, yet the worry of having another child with problems like Merrill's was naturally a cause for much concern. What should they do? It was only after a great deal of prayerful consideration that they decided that they would increase the size of their family. They felt that if the Lord wanted them to have another handicapped child, that he would surely show them the way to care for it and somehow they would find the strength to do so. It was worth the risk. Their family grew.

The Stanleys were yet to be greatly tried. Merrill became very sick and it was determined that he had pneumonia. Surely, his time had come, thought his parents. They knew it was for the best, that they had done all that could be done for him. They would accept it and let him go. But Merrill recovered from the illness, teaching his mother and father a great lesson, that it was not in their power to say what was best for Merrill, but only to give him the love and care that he needed day after day, night after night. And this is what they did.

When Merrill became older he attended the Utah Valley Care and Training Center. He was not able to do much for he was also mentally retarded, but he seemed to enjoy the companionship of the other children and his mother was able to spend more time with her young children. Things seemed to go quite well for awhile, and then when Merrill was about eight years old, a serious illness again struck him. He began to have seizures and was taken to the hospital, where he was tested for every conceivable problem—brain tumors, cerebral hemorrhage, meningitis and many other problems. The results were all negative, except that his white blood count showed an abnormality. It reached a level of 50,000. (Normal is 6,000 to 8,000; 15,000 usually means appendicitis.) The doctors could find no apparent cause for such an extreme rise in the count. They could only say, "We do not know." But the sickness left Merrill partly paralyzed, partly sightless and almost completely speechless...why? How the Stanleys wondered why.

There seemed to be no cause and no cure for the sickness from which Merrill must suffer. It all seemed too enormous, too overpowering, too completely unfair! When they took him home from the hospital, his father carried him into the house, but his mother could not bring herself to go in. "I had the overwhelming urge to run away," she said, "to search for answers, for help, for comfort. But as I ran, there came only the realization that it must all be faced, that I must cope with it, and that with effort and faith God would help me to be able to meet each day and each problem."

As time passed, Merrill's condition became increasingly worse. The family had grown, and as responsibilities grew with the children, Marilyn and Neldon were faced with an important decision which comes to all parents of severely handicapped children. Where is the best place for him? Should they have him admitted to the State Training School hospital, where he could receive constant care and proper medical attention? Should they try to keep him home with the family? The pressures of home were growing more and more intense, and though they loved Merrill very deeply, they knew—as all parents come to realize—that their full attention could not in all fairness be given to one child alone. They knew that Merrill could never be normal, that in fact, he would probably never improve in his condition. It was time now to prepare themselves to be separated from him, and eventually even for his death. But that did not come, as yet. Merrill was taken to the hospital and lay in a state of unawareness. He was well cared for and was fed often but continued to lose weight rapidly. It did not appear that he could live very long, but he lingered on for many months, and by the time he died, he was eleven years old and weighed only twenty pounds.

No one knows how much Merrill suffered, he could never tell anyone. It seemed that only his body existed in that hospital bed those many months—his mind was oblivious to all that went on around him. But perhaps, too, he realized more than we know, and suffered more than we know. Either way, death for him was surely sweet and came none too soon.

In spite of the doctor's advice to discontinue having children, the Stanleys became parents of nine children, all well and normal, with the exception of Merrill. They have also taken other children into their home and have been blessed in many ways for having done so. One might think that the many great trials they had with Merrill was cause for them to become bitter, but that is certainly not the case. They say that it has given them a much deeper awareness of what love really is and has brought them so much closer to the realization of what parenthood is all about. Marilyn feels that she has learned another great lesson, too—that we can endure to the end of our trials, whatever they might be and however difficult. Then, and only then, do we fully realize the blessings of such trials. But the blessings do come. For it is said, "Ye cannot behold with your natural eyes, for the present time, the design of your God concerning those things which shall come hereafter, and the glory which shall follow after much tribulation. For after much tribulation come the blessings." (D & C 58:3-4.)

*D*on Hundley was born to William and Vera Hundley, a family who show love and concern for each other. Don had a great talent for making the best of a problem, and seemed to have an unquenchable desire to be busily engaged in the business of living. Due to difficulties during his birth, Don was not able to do some of the things others did, but he was always making something, selling something, or helping someone, even though he faced the days with pain and uncertainty.

He participated in school activities, worked hard whenever the opportunity arose and kept his life very full of worthwhile things, proving to all that a handicap need not be a burden, if one has the right attitude.

After Don's death, his parents were awarded an honorary letter in sports, in his behalf, for his willing devotion to the Orem High School football team, where he served as manager. His friends will long remember the everlasting example he showed and the influence he had on the team.

Don was our nephew, and for the family his death has been a difficult experience, but there is no doubt in my mind that there was a purpose for his life. He was an example of great courage in the face of trial and disappointment, and though there were many things he could not do, whatever he did he did well. How great it would be if that were true of all of us.

S.A.H.

Chapter 5

From Frogs to Football

Story of Don Hundley

"Everything has its beauty, but not everyone sees it."

—Confucius

They called him Donny, until he grew too old for it—then it was Don. He was the kind of boy who let a lot of nice things find their way into his heart, and nice things always seemed to find their way out, and into the hearts of others.

Knowing Donny, someone might have said, "Oh, what a little character!" and I guess that was true. He was really full of it—full of living and loving and giving. Donny found happiness and goodness in life, in spite of some very trying experiences, but then he was like that. He made the most of what he had and enjoyed life to the fullest.

He was the fourth child born to his parents in a home where love was always strong. Don's family experienced the usual upsets and the ordinary kinds of family problems, but they were a close family and meant a great deal to him.

Birth into this world can be a simple or a traumatic thing, but either way it is a very important event in our eternal progress. To most parents it is a time of happy anticipation and joy, yet so unpredictable that there is always that element of uncertainty, even moments of fear, until we are reassured that all is well.

56

Donny's birth did not bring that reassurance. He was born feet first, with both hands above his head. The doctor had to reach in and break his left arm and shoulder. In the process, much valuable time was lost, without the precious oxygen that a baby needs.

They thought that surely he would be born dead, but he was given a shot of adrenalin and mouth-to-mouth resuscitation and was brought back to life. The doctor said that if the baby lived, chances were almost certain that he would be brain damaged. Donny's parents were told, "You'd better pray that he dies, because there is no way that he can be normal. He was too long without oxygen."

It was not Donny's parents' way to pray for him to die. He was given a blessing in the hospital, and his father watched as the tiny little boy turned from a deathly blue to a lovely pink.

Only a few hours had been given the broken little baby to live, but they passed, and after nineteen days in an incubator he was taken home, "To die," the doctors said, "there is nothing more we can do for him."

In the months that followed a close vigil was kept on the child. He could not cry aloud and was paralyzed on the left side from his shoulder down. When Donny was six months old, he developed pneumonia, and had only one third of his lung capacity working. This created many problems, but Donny somehow survived.

At eleven months of age, he was fitted with a brace on his back for support and physical therapy was recommended. The therapist did not give them much hope that Donny would walk before he was five years old, but he walked at eighteen months, typical of the prominent determination that he would display throughout his life. The doctor said he would never ride a bicycle, but he did. They said he could never play football, but he did. They had said he would not live, but he seemed determined to show them otherwise. Donny seemed to want to prove that life really was worth living.

There were many people who helped Donny in his life. His mother and father spent countless hours seeing to his care and training. Without the deep concern of his family and friends, he might have lived out his existence as a helpless cripple, undeveloped in either body or mind. He was not left in his crib and ignored, as some parents might have done with so little hope from the doctors. He was constantly shown love and affection. He was helped, encouraged, and even left alone at times with the idea of teaching him to help himself—difficult as it usually was. His two brothers taught him to walk by encouraging him to go back and forth between their beds. Sometimes he would fall, and at one time he slipped on the hardwood floor and fractured his skull, but even this did not discourage him.

There were no indications that Donny was not developing mentally, yet there was always the unknown answer to that question: Would he continue to progress and find a purpose in life?

Donny was alert and active and did most of the things that children did at his age. The doctors were amazed. How could it be, with so much against him? It was against medical knowledge that a baby born with such a lack of oxygen could not be brain damaged. They had said he would die, they had said he would never be normal. It seemed to be a miracle.

When Donny was five years old, the doctors decided to operate on his back. They fused twelve vertebrae, hoping to keep the back as straight as possible. For four months he was in a full body cast and could only lie on the floor or stand straight up. His usual show of strong will was evident, for he was not content only to lie on the floor and do nothing. Most of the time he was pleasant and happy, but there were times of unhappiness, too. The therapist said that the worst thing they could do for him would be to wait on him, that doing everything for him would make him a worse cripple than his original problems. So many times his parents turned their backs and walked away from him so that he would learn to help himself, though it was heartbreaking, and they were often criticized.

Donny started school at the normal age and did very well. He was the kind of boy who got along with everyone—well, almost everyone. If anyone tried to pick on him, he made it know that he would not stand for their trying to take advantage of him. (If anything went too far, he had two older brothers to back him up.) He was as good as anyone, though not perhaps as physically strong; he was an intellectual match for any child his age and even with many of the older ones.

One of the most interesting things I remember about Donny was his extraordinary fascination for life of any kind. He loved to go rabbit hunting with his dad, but could not bring himself to shoot a rabbit. He would put his sights on it until he got a perfect shot, but would pull to one side as he fired, deliberately missing the rabbit. No boy loved to fish more than Don, and he could catch fish when it seemed impossible. There didn't seem to be anything connected with animals or insects or reptiles that Donny didn't enjoy in some way. He liked bugs, spiders, snakes, hamsters, polliwogs, owls, frogs—and in his lifetime accumulated and owned one or more of each.

I remember the day our family was visiting at his home and Don, in his unselfish way asked, "Do you want a horny-toad?" Of course our little boys said yes, so we took one home, completely unaware that a few days later it would become the mother of thirteen squirming babies. It was a great experience for us, we all learned a lot about horny-toads, and I often wonder if Don somehow knew that it would be, even though he was not aware that the little mother was expecting. He seemed to have a kind of inner spark, the kind that shows that there is something special about a person.

His special way with animals was evident, like the time he took the thorn out of the German Shepherd's foot. The dog was so mean that even the owner used a stick to keep distance between him and the dog, and when the thorn became lodged in its foot, no one could get near it. The owner called a vet, thinking the only way to take care of the matter was to tranquilize the dog and then work on its foot. Don was about eight years old and had no fear whatsoever of animals. He went into the yard and talked to the dog, and by the time the vet arrived, Don had removed the thorn and was holding the huge paw under his arm, painting it with merthiolate.

Don was always trying to be helpful. One time a friend of his had a mare with a new colt and she wouldn't let anyone near it. They couldn't even find out whether the colt was male or female.

"I'll find out," said Don confidently, and over the fence he went. Sure enough, he got close to the colt, looked it over good and then came back.

"Well," asked the owner, "did you get close enough to find out?"

"Yeah," replied Don, "but I have one question."

"What's that?"

"How do you tell?" asked Don.

I guess most little boys want a horse of their own sometime or other in their life. Don was no exception. He loved to go to the Little Buckaroo Rodeos and one year they were giving away Shetland ponies. All you had to do was catch one and it was yours. Don figured this was his chance—he'd get one of those ponies no matter what!

But Don's will was much stronger than his body and his thoughts much faster than his feet. As he ran after the horses he tripped and fell into the path of the oncoming herd. There were about seventy horses running straight at him and it seemed there was no way he could avoid being trampled. But Don remained quiet and seemingly unafraid and the horses passed by without touching him. I'm sure Don was disappointed in not catching one, but I think that by then he had experienced many disappointments in his life, and he seemed to know how to cope with them. He also knew there would be many more. Still, he did not give up. Though his hopes and dreams were often dashed to the ground, he always seemed to have the faith and courage to get up and try again.

Helen Keller once said that if we did not struggle, we could not rest. If there were no failures, we could not know success. This could not be a pleasant world if there were no disappointments. Don had many failures, many disappointments, but he was also successful at many things. He wanted to play the games that other boys played, and though the doctors had said he must not play in regular football games, he would get a game going on his front lawn and play touch football with his brothers and friends. They all knew they must be careful not to be too rough with him, yet always let him share in their fun.

One time the ball was passed to him and when he caught it, it knocked him completely unconscious. The boys hurried to him, "Hey, Don," they said, "what happened, are you hurt?" Don opened his eyes and smiled, "Oh, I'm okay," he replied, "I just caught it in the solar plexis!"

He had only 40% of the use of his muscles, and his stomach did not have enough strength to stop a fast-moving football without it knocking the breath out of him. Actually he had no feeling in some parts of his body and at one time didn't know he had burned his stomach from leaning over the hot toaster.

Donny lived with many problems, but few of them were evident to those who saw him doing so many things. He could have been excused from physical education classes in junior high school, but he wouldn't hear of it. Even though he couldn't run around the track as fast or do the strenuous exercises that the others did, he was always in there trying, dressed in his gym suit and was part of what was going on. He was on the school newspaper staff, he ran for studentbody president, and always took part in whatever activities that he could manage.

It was not surprising that he was made manager of the high school football team. He couldn't play in the game, but no one had more enthusiasm or team loyalty than Don. He was there for every practice and every game. With his happy disposition and perpetual eagerness, he gave encouragement and hope to the team. Later his parents were awarded an honorary "letter" for football, in his behalf.

I suppose none of us will ever know how all this made Don feel—having to take the back seat, so to speak. But how many of us, when deprived of the things we want, can pleasantly step down to the next rung on the ladder and still smile? Don could. I suppose there were times when he thought about his disabilities and said, "Why me?" But I do know that from the example he set and the love he continually showed for others that he wasn't bitter about it. Perhaps at times he felt left out, but he seemed to say to himself, "I'll do the best I can each day and never waste a moment of life. I'll live the best my condition will allow me to live and meet my trials bravely. I'll find strength in one way or another—if not physically, then in my way of facing life." And that is what he did.

There is a little poem by Bernard Baruch that says:

> If you can't be a highway, just be a trail,
> If you can't be a sun, be a star,
> For it's not by the size that you win or fail,
> But by being the best of whatever you are.

From the time that Don was able to get around by himself he was always doing something to keep busy. He was either making something or selling something or working for someone. When he was five years old, he would load up his wagon with cucumbers and sell them to the neighbors. He sent for greeting cards, jewelry and other handy items to sell. He tended kids, did all kinds of handy-man jobs whenever possible, and when he was sixteen, he got a job in a service station many miles from home and was always dependable. By now his body was becoming quite deformed from the curve in his spine and his stamina was very limited.

He was active in church and community affairs, always willing to help with responsibilities, whether it be raising money for a building fund or helping in the boy scout program. At one time his group decided to raise and sell cucumbers to meet their share of the church building fund. Don brought his father and they turned the ground, planted the cucumbers and helped weed them until they were ready for harvest. The group leader said he would get up to go to work early in the mornings and see Don out working in the cucumbers. His mother helped, too, and in time they did raise the money they had pledged for the church.

Another time Don was on a trip with the scouts in the desert on a rabbit hunt. They had hunted all day and had walked for many miles. Don was tired, and when they got back to the car, they found that their leader had locked his keys in the trunk. It was January and very cold and muddy and it was at least fifteen miles to the nearest town. The leader told the boys to get in the car and stay there until he got back. He started to walk, and when he got a little ways away, he heard Don yelling at him. "Hey, wait, Gary—I'm coming with you." He had walked all day and was dog-tired. It made his leader feel more than ever that he must get to town and get help. He could surely do it, if this small, fragile boy was so willing to try. In the process, Don had given his coat to the boys in the car so they wouldn't be cold.

Don's football coach called him "great." He tells of the times when Don was asked to do things in connection with the team. Often Don had to struggle, even stumble to accomplish the task he was asked to do, but he always did it. This, he said of Don, was the mark of greatness, for he could succeed in spite of his handicaps and didn't make excuses.

His sister has said of him, "He was a loveable uncle to his nephews, taking them with him many places that he went. Very few young uncles would tolerate taking small children with them, but he took Ian fishing, night-crawler hunting, selling and just plain goofing around.

"As a young boy, Don was typically all boy. He was mischievous and he earned and received his share of punishment. He was the boy who was the apple of his Dad's eye, but the tack in the seat of his pants. Dad couldn't say anything without Don coming back with a witty remark, and even though Don couldn't play around in the rough stuff with the other boys, he yelled and cheered just as loud as anybody. He was always a part of the activities going on around him."

As time went on, it became more evident that the crippling condition of Don's body was increasing. His back was curved like the trunk of a tree that has been bent to one side by pressures of heavy snow and wind. The doctors said that his heart and lungs were becoming so crowded that he could not live in this condition for many more years. Surgery was the only answer, and there was no 100% guarantee that it would work.

At his birth, the doctors had said he would not live. When he did they said he would not be normal, yet for sixteen full years he had lived a busy life. Should he trust in their judgment now? They said the chances of survival were not good, but how much time would he have without an operation?

Benjamin Franklin once said, "Dost thou love life? Then do not squander time, for that is the stuff life is made of." It was time for Don to make the all-important decision.

This boy wanted so much to be like other boys. He wanted to be straight, to be strong, to dance with girls, to run and work and play like other young men his age. He went willingly to the hospital to have the surgery that might give him that right, knowing that it might not be successful. But it seems that Don was not meant to be like other boys. From the very beginning Donny was something special, different, outstanding.

At the hospital he was given many tests and preparations were made for the surgery.

It was the plan of the doctors to separate the fusions which had previously been made in his spine and place him in a "halo brace" which would stretch and straighten his back and keep it straight. To do this, all the ribs on one side must be broken. Two large, steel pins were placed in his skull and also in his pelvis. The brace was then to be attached to these to keep the body from curving. I cannot even imagine the courage it must have taken for this young boy to endure such torturous treatment as was inflicted upon his small, crippled body, yet he accepted and bore it in the hopes of becoming "better."

How much better could Don have been? He could not run fast, he had little strength, he could not hike like other boys, yet in his lifetime accomplished more than many ever accomplish. His strength existed in his character, in his love of life, and in his shining example to everyone who knew him. When we feel that sometimes we have problems to bear, when pain and discomfort plague our body and make us down-hearted, when uncertainty and wonder bring questions about the future, we ought to think of Don.

He seemed to travel through life knowing that a famous sea captain once said, "A smooth sea never made a skillful mariner. The storms of adversity, like those of the ocean, rouse the faculties and excite the invention, skill, prudence and fortitude of the voyager." It seems so true of many people with handicaps that the rougher the sea, the better the sailor.

Don didn't make it through the operation. Our telephone rang early one morning and got us out of bed, and his father's voice came falteringly through the wire. "My boy is dead," he said, "My boy is dead." Don's death has been difficult for his family and we all miss him and the great example that he set, but Don is not dead. I feel about him as I do of David, that because of his love and strength of character, our Father in Heaven has seen a greater need for him in another place, where he is surely as actively engaged as he was here. He has only gone on before us, not left us forever. It is as Longfellow has written:

> Thou hast taken up thy lamp
> and gone to bed:
> I stay a little longer,
> as one stays
> To cover up the ashes that still burn.

Don and David were cousins. Both—in spite of their different handicaps—brought something worthwhile and wonderful into the lives of all those who knew them. Don proved that even though life is a great challenge, we can carry our burden, however hard. We can work, even though we find it difficult, and that we can bring happiness to others if we will only put forth the effort.

If, by some miracle, like the one at the time of Don's birth, we have gained even the smallest amount of patience, understanding, love or humility from having Don and David in our midst for a few years, then it has been worth the price we had to pay. We shall know that even though their lives were not long and they did not have the opportunity to marry and raise families of their own, still their lives were not fruitless or without great value. We shall know that they did not live—or die—in vain.

I Walked With You

I walked with you
Upon life's path,
And learned the meaning
    of God's love.
You showed me how
To look for happiness
In things that seemingly were small
And unimportant in my life.
And now your precious smile
Is just a memory, and yet
    a guiding light
Which leads me on
Toward the place
Where you have gone.
I want to walk with you again,
    along new paths,
And feel the warmth and beauty
    of your love,
Which glows unceasingly
Like His
Who gave me you.

—Sherrie A. Hundley

*L*ouise Baird became the mother of twins. During her pregnancy, she was stung by a bee, from which a serious allergic reaction developed. One of the babies was only slightly affected, but as the two children grew up together, Jim and Louise watched the gap grow wider and wider as one sister developed normally and one did not.

The Bairds then became faced with many ordeals, among them the decision of whether or not to place the handicapped child in an institution. Janet was diagnosed as having severe mental deficiency with cerebral palsy, and it became impossible for her to withstand the emotional challenges of a large family.

The Bairds felt that placing her in the State Training School for the Retarded was the answer to her needs. She does well in that environment and appears to be happy there. Mrs. Baird tells of the feelings of the other children in the family and of the affect that Janet's condition has had on them. They now accept it as a part of their lives, but that acceptance did not come quickly or easily.

K.J.K.

Chapter 6

The Bee Sting

Story of Janet Baird

"There is no grief which times does not lessen."

—Cicero

The most important day in our daughter Janet's life occurred before she was born. An allergic reaction from a bee sting during my pregnancy with Janet and her twin sister left her severely brain damaged. Fortunately, her twin was only mildly affected. Perhaps it was because we had a normal baby to compare her with, but we knew something was wrong with Janet from the day she was born. Still the doctor pronounced her "within the range of normal" on each checkup until she was five months old, when he finally agreed with us that something was indeed seriously wrong.

I think two things helped us accept Janet's condition in that first year without any real emotional difficulty. First, there was never a sudden shock of realization that she would not be normal. We told the doctor before he told us. Since we never had any false hopes about her condition, we were never let down. The second help was that her twin sister was growing normally and filling in the gap of disappointment we might have felt at being cheated out of the relationship with the baby we had hoped and planned for.

During Janet's second and third years our pediatrician advised that it was time to seek additional help. We took Janet first to a neurologist, then to a specialist in physical medicine, and finally to an orthopedic specialist. All the information we received merely reinforced what our doctor had already diagnosed—Janet had cerebral palsy, and was severely mentally retarded. We faithfully followed all the prescriptions, including tranquilizers and two weekly trips to Salt Lake for physical therapy. We also spent many hours exercising at home with her. Never did we suppose that our efforts would work miracles, but there was some progress and, most of all, the assurance of knowing that if anything could be done for her we were doing it.

Finally, when she was four we realized that the pressures of living in a home filled with noisy, normal children was becoming emotionally impossible for Janet. I was pregnant with another set of twins and it became extremely difficult for me to care for her. She was accepted at the Utah State Training School three months before her fifth birthday, and there she has lived ever since. She is now almost ten and her physical and mental condition has changed very little in that time. We are grateful for the loving care of those who work with her at the Training School. She is clean, happy, and violently unhappy anywhere else. She has been given intensive sensory motor training, but it has produced very little in lasting development. Again we are comforted in knowing that all that could be done for her has been done.

Janet's membership in our family has affected our children in various ways. We have two children older than Janet, her twin, and five younger children. The three youngest have been born since Janet left our home. None of the five youngest children remember any relationship with her except in our visits to the school. They know she is their sister and they love to go to see her, but she has never really been a family member to them. It is interesting, though, that even these little ones seem to display an unusual compassion not only for Janet but also for the other children at the Training School. They are not shocked by even the most grotesque disabilities they see there.

Our oldest boy, Glen, was seven when Janet left. He was very upset, threatening to get up early in the morning and take Janet up into the hills and hide her so that we couldn't take her away. He has always been gentle and tender, but very matter-of-fact about her condition. When his friends stared at her misshapen body, he simply explained, "That's my sister Janet. She's brain-damaged and can't play." Now that he's older he continues to accept people with handicaps and differences with compassion and understanding.

Janet's condition affected our oldest daughter, Joanne, very deeply, but it was not until after Janet left our home that we realized how much. Looking back, we remembered that Joanne hardly interacted with Janet at all. She almost behaved as though Janet didn't exist. The first time we took the family to visit Janet at the Training School Joanne went to sleep in the car, or pretended to sleep, to avoid seeing her. This happened several times and it took us a long time and much gentle persuasion to help Joanne to accept Janet and enjoy visiting her. Now that Joanne is older we have been able to talk about those early years and how she felt. She was not uncaring, but frightened by concerns she could not cope with or talk about. Joanne is a sensitive, loving child and the fact that Janet did not get any better no matter what we did, made her feel helpless and frustrated.

Janet's twin, Christine, also has had tremendous concern for Janet, but she has been able to verbalize her fears. Christine has strong faith and feels a sense of eternal responsibility for her twin sister. Her goal in life is to live righteously so that some day she and Janet can live together with both of them whole and normal. Christine expects to teach the gospel to Janet and to share eternity with her.

As Janet's parents, we have experienced a variety of emotions in our relationship with Janet. Certainly our religious faith has been the foundation of all we have felt. We have also had the support of a compassionate and competent pediatrician, caring people at the Training School, our parents, brothers and sisters and kind friends. We have experienced a profound love for our little girl which is difficult to describe. Our joy with her has been more acceptance than hope, more sweetness than fun, more quiet watching than active participation, more patience than pride.

As the years pass, Janet affects the lives of the rest of our children less and less, as we get caught up in all the other things we have to do with a large family. Each year it becomes more difficult to include her in our thinking and planning for our family. We realize that it is an enormous challenge to make her life important to her brothers and sisters so that in that distant day when she takes her place with the rest of us she will not be a stranger. We are confident that our daughter is in the right place and doing the right thing. Her life is motivation for the rest of us to do the same.

PERPETUAL CHILDREN

God loves the children, and he sent a few
Who would throughout this life remain childlike,
Blessed with that innocence, itself a grace
Too soon outgrown. The likes of me and you
Cannot return. We hear the hour strike
And move with it, struggle to keep apace.

Perpetual children have a favored place
In earth and heaven; earth because, unlike
The restless throng, they are assured of love,
And need not go a-seeking. Heaven-like,
They are redeemed already, good as new,
Because they know no sin. Celestial love,
That all-encompassing, all-knowing love
Pre-tested these—and knew they would come through!

Yet in an after-world, their childhood lifted,
These might emerge more talented, more gifted
Than some of us who strove to make a score—
We cannot measure what has gone before.
It may be that He sent these favored few
To show us what perpetual love can do.

——Ora Pate Stewart

Dr. Glen Brown is well-known in the Provo, Utah area for his many years of service in the field of education. He began his career as a teacher in the Provo City schools and became a principal the same year that his son, Mike, was stricken with polio. Glen and his wife, Betty, spent endless hours with Mike, through his years of rehabilitation as well as the hardship of the disease. It was through teaching Mike to swim that Glen became interested in helping to develop a program for other handicapped children throughout Utah County.

Dr. Brown has worked as Administrative Director of the Youth Center at the Utah State Hospital and is now Executive Director of the Timpanogos Mental Health Center. He was bishop of a B.Y.U. branch for six years and has given many lectures explaining his views on the meaning of life and the thrill of existence.

Mrs. Brown, he says, is the "real star of the show." Not the kind to take the bows, she is a solid, supportive part of the family, withstanding the intense time pressure required for the care of Mike and the other six children in the family, and holding various positions in the church. At the same time, she has always encouraged her husband to go out and do the things which have made him a very successful person.

The Browns are very proud of Mike for what he has been able to achieve in his young life. Though he walks only with the aid of a brace or crutches, he is able to take great strides in accomplishing what he sets out to do. He lives by the code that his handicap will never keep him from anything if he wants it badly enough. He has graduated from college and is now working for a master's degree. He is involved with swimming intramurals, has won arm wrestling championships, and has completed a mission for the L.D.S. Church. He was recently able to go to Washington, D.C., where he worked with Congressman Gunn McKay and also for I.B.M. You may even see Mike Brown on the ski slopes. He ties his bad leg behind him, puts on one ski, and using his "outrigger" crutches—away he goes! Mike knows he will never be a great skier, as he knows he will never be a track star, but he says that doesn't matter, because there are so many other things which he can enjoy and excel in. His success proves that he is right.

S.A.H.

Chapter 7

The Power of Love

Story of Mike Brown

"When love and skill work together, expect a master-piece."
                                                    —John Ruskin

Many years ago a large number of children became afflicted with a crippling disease called polio, or infantile paralysis. Some died from its terrible effects, and of those who survived, many were paralyzed for life or crippled in some way.

Among these was a small boy named Michael Brown, who for more than twenty-two years has worked with his disablement and has proved that one can still walk the road of life, even with a useless leg. With the love and patience of his parents and others, Mike has been able to gain strength and independence, and has developed a great outlook on life.

The Father's Story:

"I remember it so vividly. This kind of thing never leaves you, I guess. Mike was just two years old and had always been tre-mendously active. We noticed he had a runny nose and a small fever, and when I was painting the house I saw him fall. Later, he refused to walk, and when the doctor had examined him he said, 'The signs aren't too strong, but it looks like polio'.

"They took a spinal tap to be sure. We weren't in the room, but we could hear little Mike screaming, and when it was all over, the doctor announced to us, 'Your boy has polio'."

Mike lay in his father's arms and watched the tears drop down on his blanket. "Don't cry, Daddy," he said as he looked up at his sorrowing father. His mother was very solid, but when they reached home, she too, began to cry. It was more than they felt they could bear. A two-year-old lad wiped out, it seemed, yet his little eyes were bright and his voice was strong. Inside was an excellent mind, but outside was a body that couldn't move.

"We did as the doctors told us," Glen related. "We trusted in them completely. The boy was isolated for quite some time, and even after the tremendous onslaught of the disease was over, the muscle atrophy and the racking pain were vicious. Finally, it was over and the rehabilitation had to begin."

Mike was taken home from the hospital, and the therapy, the feeding and the diaper changing were all continued exactly as the doctors had told them. They also concentrated very strongly on his personality development and their relationship with them. Even though it was heartbreaking to them, *Mike* wasn't heartbreaking to them.

"That initial shock was a disastrous one," said Glen. "Many nights I cried myself to sleep, thinking my wife didn't know. Now and then I would feel her arm touch mine, as she gave me that quiet support. I suppose she was crying, too."

At all times the Browns prayed and tried the best they could to cope with their problems. They come from a large family, who all rallied to their need, giving them social and spiritual support which was very helpful.

"I guess foremost were those good medical men," explains Dr. Brown, "tougher than bears! I didn't understand it at first—I thought they were being cruel—but when I caught the vision of what they were doing, then I was able to find a light in my life again and happiness in the world. I was able to do the things they told me to do.

"As we watched Mike's personality develop," he continued, "it was a precious time in our lives. I think that's the joy that is spoken of in the scriptures that a man is to have joy. It's the joy of accomplishment, the joy of overcoming, the joy of having been to the brink and then returning."

As Mike went through the disease and he got through the initial trial and learned to face it, there were tremendous adjustments to make. Glen was principal of an elementary school and he and Betty were very busy people. They also loved to spend time in the out-doors, to hike and camp, and they loved to play ball, but a lot of these things had to change. First, this young child had to be taken care of. Glen and Betty felt that the Lord had sent him to them and he was their first responsibility. So they had to get up a little earlier, and after breakfast, came the one hour of therapy—every day for nine years, except on Sundays and special holidays. It had to be done in a certain prescribed way, including putting on the steel-canvas corset that Mike had to wear. At night he had to be laced in bed and tied in a certain position. It was not easy, but his parents felt that they were doing something to help him. Now they didn't have that lost, hopeless feeling, because they were a part of it.

"The key to the handicapped is *do,*" says Dr. Brown. "The best thing for the individual and the people around him is to get involved. Don't stand there and cry in your handkerchief—get them doing something!"

There were, of course, periods of time that were really rough, like the first time Mike went to school, dragging his brace. His father remembers, "It was a hard thing to accept, the fact that he'd have to drag that brace all his life, but he has done it. He faces people that don't understand him and he faces their false pity or their over-attention. Because of it he is a tremendous man...tremendous inside."

The Brown's went on doing many of the things they liked to do. They went deer hunting and Glen would carry Mike on his back up the mountain. Sometimes Glen's brothers would take a turn, they were always involved. Glen would insist that Mike do as much as he was able, and many times he watched as Mike struggled up the mountain, grabbing at roots and literally crawling to get where he wanted to go.

Even a year before Mike went on his mission at nineteen years of age, they took a trip down the Snake River. Mike couldn't wear his brace in the canoe, so when they would get out, his father would carry him on his back, Mike weighing 175 pounds. "I could carry him because I've carried him all my life," related Glen. "Sometimes I'd say, 'Would you stop choking me?' and he'd reply, 'Okay, if you'll go faster!' This was the kind of relationship we enjoyed together."

Much of Glen and Betty's time alone was spent talking about their situation, sharing their feelings and discussing possible solutions to their problems. They never tried to hide it or gloss over it. When they felt a frustration or a difficulty, they always talked about it, sometimes with close friends or family members, but never isolating themselves from society. When people would ask how he was doing, however, they would usually answer and then the subject was changed.

Dr. Brown says they made many mistakes, but he explains that it is very unrealistic for parents to think they can be successful all the time. Even with normal children we can't be totally successful, because we don't understand it all. Much of life is experimental, but the main thing to do when you're coping with a problem such as theirs is to *"insist on the enjoyment of the challenge as an individual, at whatever level he's at, and enjoy him.* It's all you've got."

"I guess the most important thing we did," Dr. Brown continues, "was to continually express—physically, as well as vocally—the love we had for Mike and how proud we were that the Lord had sent him to our family. There was a continual round of reinforcement, and we tried not to let negativism ever enter in.

We did not ignore the fact that he could not do some things, but we would continually tell him, 'We love you, you are successful, you can do it.' Then we watched very carefully and tried to be realistic when he couldn't do some things. You have to look for what they *can* do, and that is what you focus on."

The Browns found that Mike could handle himself very well in the water. So they got him into the swimming pools and this was where Glen pioneered a program of recreation for other handicapped kids in the county. Mike was the germ of the idea. They taught kids to swim and enjoy themselves in ways they could never have done otherwise, and Mike became one of the instructors, even though he had to hop around the pool.

"But Mike was not always this successful in the things he tried," his father remembers. "The first time he went to try out for little league baseball, I watched him lunge and knock down a line drive and then crawl in the dirt, dragging his brace, and I was full of tears, because I could see that he couldn't play baseball. I knew it, but he didn't, and so he tried. The coach wouldn't put him on the team, and Mike went home and cried for hours that day. I tried to be very loving and consoling, and finally Mike was able to see that we all have to realize our limitations and do the best with what we've got.

"You have to have some great emotional strengths yourself in order to allow a child to develop to his fullest. You've got to let him be himself, and in being himself, he has to have room for a degree of failure, as well as success. Failure may be too final a word, let's call it disappointment. To be a winner, you have to have the right to lose. We have to expect this with anyone, but especially a handicapped child. Respect his right to have disappointment, but always bolster him."

For instance, Glen recalls when Mike started to walk. "It was impossible—no muscles in the stomach to speak of, no muscles in the buttocks, no muscles in the leg. Maybe a flicker or two, that was all. Then the muscles began to develop and he found a way to sling the brace. But he would fall and then he'd have to get up. It would have been so easy for me to pick him up, but I knew I wasn't going to be with him all his life. So I would turn my back and listen to his pleas, 'Help me, Daddy, help me,' but I would have to ignore him, insisting that he get up himself. I tried to understand his problem; I tied splints on my leg, but that wasn't accurate because I had muscles. I couldn't even imagine what Mike was going through, yet I had to insist that he do it himself. He would drag himself across the floor, start up the leg of a table or chair and then jacknife his butt into the air. Then he would bring his hands up the brace until he was standing. He learned, I didn't teach him. I gave him the opportunity to learn, and when he'd get through, I'd say, 'You're great!'"

When Mike was in high school he decided to go into wrestling, but one day a disastrous thing happened to him. He was quite a vocal boy and he had been telling everyone he could beat the kid he was going to wrestle. He was very confident. But they hadn't gone thirty seconds into the match when Mike was pinned. He didn't beat the kid, he didn't even get a decision, he was pinned. He was defeated in front of his friends, and to Mike it meant that he was defeated in life. They held up the winner's hand and even though Mike was trying to be a good sport, you could see that he was psychologically crushed.

"I watched as Michael hopped out of the gym," his father said, "down the staircase and into oblivion. It wasn't fair for a lad to be ashamed when he was doing his best. I got up and left the gym and found Mike sitting in the locker room."

"How you doin'?" Glen asked. And then Mike exploded! He inflicted himself with terrible self-criticism—how lousy he was, how stupid! He was absolutely vicious.

"When he finally ran down," his father remembers, "I said: You have a couple of choices, as I see it, son. One is to get your tail up where you belong and support your team. The other is to get into that shower and quit and I'll take you home."

Mike's eyes flashed and he fairly screamed, "I'M NO QUITTER!"

"Then get up there where you belong," his Dad told him, and then he walked out of the locker room.

In his own way, Glen was telling him I love you, I support you, you're worthwhile, now act like it.

Mike did have the courage to go up the stairs and get back on the bench. He later said that the way his dad handled the situation had a marvelous effect on him. It made him see how important it was for him to think of his responsibilities. He'd been thinking, "If only I'd had two good legs like the other guy..." His Dad taught him that life has to go on no matter what.

"My whole life has been like that," says Mike. "My dad has taught me that there is no such thing as an excuse. I couldn't play baseball but I learned to play marbles, and I won the championship of my school two years in a row. I even made football one year. When Provo High took second in the State I considered myself a very important part of the team. I wasn't just the manager, I was Mike Brown, and they asked me for advice and treated me as an equal. They smacked me on the back the same as they smacked the guy who made the touchdown, and that was very exciting for me. Those guys had a very strong influence on my life, and I will always be grateful to them."

Mike has faced many good things and many bad things in his life. He has also had many difficulties to work out because he walks differently than you and I. He is a gregarious, happy, outgoing person on the outside, but on the inside he has problems just like anyone else. When he was in junior high school he came home one evening and wouldn't talk to anyone. His father went to his room and tried to engage in conversation, but Mike was quiet. Finally he blurted out, "It's Steve. He calls me Pegleg and Limpy and other nasty names."

His father quietly talked for a few minutes and then asked, "What do you want to do, son?"

"I want to beat the devil out of him," replied Mike.

"Mike," his father continued, "if you fight and learn to solve your problems by fighting you'll suffer all your life, because you'll win very few. This kid will probably beat you because he'll hit and then run, and all you'll do is grow up to be a bitter, frustrated individual. I don't want you to fight."

"But, Dad, what'll I do?" Mike's voice was pleading.

"Have you ever looked closely at this kid, Mike?" asked his father. "...bright eyes, beautiful hair...his name is really *Stephanie,* Mike."

There was a moment of silence. "Goodnight, Dad. I'll see you in the morning."

The next day Mike went to his Dad. "Steve came pumping up on his bike today, Dad," he said, "with his Iron Leg and vicious names, and I called out, 'Oh, Stephanie, you beautiful thing. Who does your hair?' He wheeled around on his bike and got close to me and I grabbed him. I said, 'You lay off and I lay off,' and it was over."

Mike didn't have to fight that time. He made his point vocally and by the strength in his grab (his hands and arms are very strong.) That boy and Mike have been the greatest of friends all their lives.

Dr. Brown has helped his son to find many successes in life and has also had a great deal of experience working with other young people. We asked him to tell us what he would say to someone who might come to him for advice if they had a handicapped child. He said:

"You have lots of children with handicaps, because everyone is your child, everyone is your brother. Maybe now it has come closer to you and you say 'Why me?' Handicapped children have been around for a long time, but now one of them has come into your house to live with you.

"I think about Job in the Bible, and the Lord said, 'Where wast thou when I laid the foundations of the earth?' We were there just as Job was there and we knew what it was going to be like on earth, but we said 'Send Me down, Lord, I can't progress any more without a body.' We knew there would be disappointments and trials but we wanted to come anyway. So we came down here, and all of a sudden we find that this physical clay is not perfect, and we may think of it as a tragedy. But it isn't a tragedy when we have a special child. It's our love for him that's important."

Dr. Brown continues, "But I had desires for this child, you say. You are wallowing in self-pity. Maybe there is a great lesson for you to learn and it will be very difficult unless you can conquer your feelings. You must love this handicapped child, accept him, enjoy him and don't be threatened by him. Don't flaunt him in front of people, but let people help you, even if for a time it means putting the child in an institution. Institutions were made to help. There is no need to feel guilty. Go about your activities of having a happy life and avoid sitting and crying about your problems.

"Now, I can talk that way because my boy has only a physical problem. Mentally, he is healthy and happy and has a good outlook on life. But with any kind of handicapped person, you need to be gentle, be supportive, learn all you can and be proud that the Lord is testing you. Sometimes when I am blue I talk to people who are close to me. They may not even know they are helping me, but friends can be one of your greatest supports. So surround yourself with good friends and most of all, let God be your friend. If you can do that, you'll make it."

The Son's Story:

Mike says that the beauty of his life is that even though he has walked with a crippled leg, he doesn't feel that life has been so different for him. He credits this happy situation to his faithful parents, who have helped him fill his life so full of the enjoyable and good things that his problems have been only a minor part of it. Parents like his are invaluable and he says he can't imagine what he would be without them, for they have made him what he is. They taught him to look beyond his crippled leg and never let it get in his way. He explains:

"My life is simply too important to me to let anything interfere with it. I love life and I love the opportunities I have to associate with the wonderful people I have met. One of the greatest things in my life has been my friends.

"I have always tried to keep myself very active. There are many people who have something physically wrong and they just let themselves deteriorate. They become so withdrawn that their physcial handicap creates an emotional handicap as well. I've seen things go wrong with people physically and it has taken them away from their belief in God. I refuse to let that happen to me. Having a handicap just can't be that big of a deal! There are lots of things in life that are worse than having a bad leg or being blind or losing an arm. A physical handicap is much easier to overcome than a mental, spiritual or emotional handicap. I feel I am very lucky, because all I have is a physical handicap.

"I think the toughest period in a person's life is when they are in grade school and up through high school. The physical things are so important. It's always, "who's the best at playing games or who's going to make the team?" Even the girls are more interested in the boys who are in athletics. I had to learn that and adapt to it or let it beat me. I could have just gone into a shell and withered up, but I decided to learn to make the best of it.

"I had an excellent childhood. I learned very young that if I was in a game where my lack of speed or ability hindered me, I would either get in a position where I could minimize it or I would simply change the game. I came up with a kind of crawling football. You literally had to crawl to play, and it became one of the favorite games of all the kids in the neighborhood.

"I'll never forget some of the lessons I learned in wrestling. I made up my mind that my useless leg would never hold me back, and so I developed my arms and the upper half of my body to compensate. One of the toughest things I had to do was to get myself dressed in those wrestling tights and then without the use of my brace, hop out in front of all those people who were staring at me and wondering what I was doing in an athletic event. After wearing a brace all your life, you don't realize how you look to other people—to those who aren't your friends and have grown accustomed to your withered leg. So I had to adjust to that, or give up, and I wasn't willing to do that.

"I learned a lot from my first wrestling match. I was only a sophomore and my opponent was a senior with a leather jacket that had 'All-State Champion for Two Years' on it. There I was, my first match and it was against this great, awesome wrestler. I felt like backing out, but I went in there and did my best. I didn't win the match, but I didn't get pinned, and after it was over, this great wrestler told me that I was really good and that he was glad to have been my opponent. I was really glad that I hadn't quit.

"So I found out that by just doing my best with what I had, I could gain a great deal of satisfaction and a feeling of success, even when I didn't win, and all these things had a lot of influence on my life."

There are many other experiences which have also had a direct influence on Mike's life. He says that growing up with his brother, Barry, has been a beautiful experience. They have always been extremely close and have done some crazy, fun things together. When kids would make fun of Mike's crippled leg, Barry would challenge them, either in a bicycle race or something else. He was always there to help Mike, and Mike wondered how he could ever repay Barry. Many times Barry would put his own personal welfare on the line for Mike.

One of these times was at a hockey game where Mike had gone with Barry and some friends. There was a red-headed guy there with a very foul mouth and he said things that were very unpleasant. He kept calling Mike "the cripple" and said he would meet him outside after the game.

Mike wasn't ready to go out and fight; he didn't like that sort of thing. He remembered what his dad had taught him about fighting and how you never really win that way. But the guy kept calling him names and when they got outside he started shoving Mike and then kicking him when he was down. It was then that Barry stepped up and told the guy to either fight like a man or else deal with him. That gave Mike a chance to stand up against the wall where the guy couldn't push him over. In Mike's words:

"When he came at me again I was ready and I stood my ground. I hit him and knocked him down and I kept hitting him until he said 'that's enough!' He went to the locker room to clean up, and I had such an awful feeling—I was sick inside for what I had had to do, but there are times in your life when you just have to prove you're a man, silly as it may seem to someone else.

"I wanted to go and put my arm around this guy and say, 'sorry this had to happen, let me help you. Let me be your friend.' I checked on him to make sure he was okay, but I'll never forget him. Neither will I forget how my brother stepped in to help me. He could have really gotten into trouble, because the other guy had some pretty big friends with him.

"Barry and I have always had that kind of bond between us, and he didn't let me down when I needed him."

Not too long ago there was a situation in their lives where Mike and Barry became even closer. Barry's arm was injured in an accident where he worked, and though it was a tragic and sad time for all the family, in a way it was one of the most beautiful experiences of Mike's life. He was finally able to do something for Barry which Barry had been doing for him all his life. The family spent what seemed like an eternity waiting to see what the outcome would be after the arm was so severely crushed. Finally, the doctors decided that the hand and part of the arm would have to be amputated. They all knew that it would be a difficult time for Barry.

"I think it was a much harder experience for him to face than my going through life with a bad leg," Mike has said. "I had grown up with mine for as long as I could remember. This came to Barry so suddenly and he had his life yet ahead of him.

"I spent a lot of time with him right after the accident, but I knew that the strength he needed from me would come later when he was recovering. I remember how I gained strength in life through the difficult days after my polio was over. When you're sick you need compassionate people around you, but when you start to get better and have something to overcome, you need strong-willed people to show you the road.

"I wanted to be Barry's strength, as Barry had so often been mine. I wanted to return to him some of the support and deep love that he had always given me, and that's the part that was so beautiful to me. We were able to share something together that perhaps no one else could ever understand."

Mike says he refuses to let Barry get down about his arm, nor use it for an excuse. They play racquet ball, they go swimming, Barry even plays on a basketball team. Mike says, "I can't say how much it has helped me to be able to help Barry. You know, you forget yourself when you're in the service of others."

One of the toughest things Mike has had to work with was the feeling that a girl could never like him because of his handicap. He was afraid that a girl would be ashamed of him and would think that he couldn't make a living. Mike has learned to overcome that fear by choosing some very special girls to go out with, girls who are very accepting and understanding, but it was rough to realize that some girls would rather not go out with him. He doesn't worry about it now, but looks forward to the day when he finds that special lovely girl and gets married.

Mike doesn't worry about making a living, either. For awhile he had a great lack of confidence in that area. Then he had a wonderful experience in Washington, D.C. which helped him overcome that lack of confidence. He was able to get a job with IBM after he had been told that there was a great number of people applying for the job. He was interviewed and hired, and it was a great victory for Mike, a great confidence builder.

Serving a mission for his church has also given Mike many growing experiences. He says he gained a great deal of spiritual strength and was able to help many others do the same. He learned what he could do with his personality and he shared his personal insights and experiences with people with whom he worked. His mission president believed as Mike's father does, that the Lord and Mike sat down together and decided before he came to this earth that he would have a handicap, and that if he used it right, it would not only be a strength to him but to others, too.

"I believe that my greatest strength lies in my love for others," Mike says, "for my family and friends and for life itself. Life has been a great training period for me, in which I have grown physically and spiritually. One of the most pleasing things

I have learned is that *there is value in everyone,* if we will just take the time to look for it. I know that if I have the right attitude that it doesn't matter what my physical body is like, my strengths can neutralize my weaknesses and make them unimportant."

Mike has come a long way since his bout with polio. He fought the pain, the frustrations, the tiring therapy and the endless hours of struggling to be able to do things that came easily for other boys. But his handicap is not a serious thing in his life. Sure he'd like to have another good leg, just as Barry would like to have his other arm, but it's not going to slow either of them down. Mike has been able to accomplish just about anything he's ever really wanted to do. He's done things that people have said there was no way he could do them, and it makes him feel good to prove that they are wrong. Not that he hasn't been a bit lazy at times, too. Self-discipline was something he always had to work on, but when he realized it, he was able to do something about it.

Mike says it's a good thing he wasn't a pioneer who had to walk across the plains, but he has been able to make do with what he has. "So what if I can't run the hundred-yard dash?" he says. "I'll get there—it will just take me a little longer."

And while he's going, Mike probably will see a lot of things which the rest of us pass by, with our two good legs.

*S*tan and Vicki Taylor *were* among those who never thought that they would ever be parents of a handicapped child. When their little Johnny was born and they were told that he had Down's Syndrome, or Mongolism, and would be mentally retarded, the idea was more than difficult to accept. They knew little of such a condition for they had never been associated with this type of child. It was something that only happened to other people.

Yet Johnny has become a source of joy and a shining light in their lives, contrary to those first fears and disappointments which the Taylors experienced upon learning of his irreversible condition. Their story is told in the words of Mrs. Taylor, from an interview, as it was mainly she who brought out their feelings concerning this child.

At the present time, Dr. Taylor is working in Washington, D.C., having been nominated by a U. S. Senator for a position on the Senate Intelligence Committee. Previously an associate professor in political science at Brigham Young University, he has also served as president of the board of directors of the symphony in Provo, Utah, and was administrative assistant to Congressman Gunn McKay. Mrs. Taylor has also shared her many talents—musical and otherwise—in various positions in church leadership. Her deep love for the gospel and for people has helped her to live successfully with what could have been an unconquerable problem—the raising of a handicapped child.

The Taylors have learned, as have others, that handicapped children come to all kinds and all classes of people. It is only when these people, whatever their status in life, can overcome the fear and anxiety of such an experience and come through with the marvelous attitude that the Taylors have—only then can they make something which seems like a disaster, not really so bad after all.

S.A.H.

Chapter 8

Our Loveable Johnny

Story of Johnny Taylor

"Love is always associated with and manifest through service." —Bruce R. McConkie

Johnny was our fifth child. The other four were all completely normal and healthy, good students, in fact just the opposite of retarded. But our Johnny has Down's Syndrome—or Mongolism. This was in no way revealed to me during my pregnancy. While I carried Johnny, he was very active, although toward the end he was not quite as active as my other babies had been.

There were no indications during delivery of any problems, but right after delivery my obstetrician asked me who my pediatrician was, and he seemed anxious to get one right away. He must have had reason to believe that something was wrong.

He came into my room later but I was sleeping and did not get to talk to him that day. The nurse brought Johnny to me, and it was thrilling to hold this new little baby. I'm so grateful for that one day with him, feeling that this was another normal baby. His facial characteristics did not reveal his condition to my unsuspecting eye. I noticed that there was a slight slant to his eyes, but passed it off as merely the result of the headsqueezing experience at birth.

85

The next morning the doctor came in again. He was very blunt. "Mrs. Taylor," he said, "we have reason to believe that your baby isn't entirely normal."

I don't think that I heard anything he said for the next few minutes. My mind was trying to grasp what he had told me. I continued to have this problem for the next few weeks—an experience of disbelief and trying to get the situation etched in my mind. I felt like a computer which had been fed some information, but I wanted to send that information back and say, "not accurate, not complete." I could not get on top of it and accept it.

The doctor was very kind. He explained to me that every one has certain characteristics which result from a normal amount of chromosomes in the body, but that when too many of these chromosomes are present it causes a condition known as Down's Syndrome. When I asked him what that meant, he said Mongolism, and then I knew with that terrible certainty that it was something bad. I had always had the darkest of feelings about Mongoloid children, coming mainly from ignorance and having no association with retarded people.

The next thing to face was telling my husband. I called and asked him to come to the hospital, and that I needed to talk to him. It was a strange feeling to know that I had actually given birth to an abnormal child—a *retarded* child! And no one knew but me.

My husband came. We paced up and down the hospital corridor and talked about our problem. We were, to say the least, very low and very depressed, very saddened by it.

We had another doctor examine Johnny. His findings were the same. He told us to take the child home, treat him like any other child in the family, and love him. He said that the more love this type of child received—the more he is treated as a normal child—the better he is and the more he will advance.

We were so grateful for this kind of advice. It oriented our thinking right from the beginning and has influenced our decision about Johnny. Another doctor was called in Salt Lake City and he advised that we put Johnny in an institution and never see him again.

Still another doctor suggested that when Johnny got his first cold that we just not treat it. These children do not have much resistence or ability to fight illness.

So you can see the wide divergence of opinions among doctors. However, we did not, at any time, consider taking the advice of the doctor who had suggested putting Johnny in an institution. Having him that one day without knowing that he was not normal was a blessing to me. I fell deeply in love with this sweet precious little baby, and finding out that he was retarded did not change my feelings in any way. We both loved him so deeply that we knew we wanted to keep him with us in our home.

We hoped that Johnny would somehow be all right, that perhaps someone had made a mistake. There were indications that he was not normal, but it was not until some time after we had taken him home that we got the results of the chromosomes count, and then we knew irrevocably that he had Down's Syndrome and would definitely be retarded.

The important thing now is to inform all of our family about our baby—the adult members—to see if they could accept this little abnormal child into the family circle. We also needed to tell our children about the situation. That was a very difficult time for all of us. When we told our eleven year old boy, he said, "If anyone ever says anything about Johnny, do you care if I beat them up?" This was the best way he had of expressing his love and his willingness to defend his little brother.

The strongest feeling that I had, as a mother, was that of absolute hopelessness. I couldn't believe that our Father in Heaven would want this sweet little baby to grow up in darkness, with no hope of opportunity to develop and learn and understand. This was very difficult for me to grasp. Feelings came into my heart that I must constantly plead with the Lord, and I would think of that song that says, "Hear my cry, hear my cry...." We loved this precious little soul so much that we continued to pray that the Lord would help us with our problem.

We had several blessings for Johnny, and while I don't think at any time we felt that there was a major miracle happening, we did feel that there was a kind of strength coming out and going into him. He is, in many ways, sweeter, cuter, and more loveable than any of our children, and he does not seem to be as severely retarded as we thought.

Just before Johnny was born we had been reading in the scriptures about how Christ had healed many little children. With this background in our minds we felt that the thing to do was to fast and pray for our son, and it was after this that it was made known to us in a very special way that Johnny was the way the Lord wanted him to be. We now knew that he was definitely going to always be retarded, and that we must accept it and try to make the best of it.

However, there were still many difficult times. For the first few months of Johnny's life it was very hard for me to get together with my neighbor who had had a baby just two days after I had. When I watched her baby starting to roll over, to crawl, to grab things, and Johnny was still content to just lie in my arms and look around, it was heart-breaking for me. I was glad that he could smile and seemed happy, but I could see the gap had widened more all the time. Finally, at about six or seven months, the gap had widened enough that it was clear that he was never going to be able to compete with other children. Our hopes of getting him into the public schools and participating in other activities with normal children were gone. We finally accepted reality, that his life would always be different, and only then was I able to stop comparing him with other children. Once I made it over this hump, I blossomed in the acceptance and realization of it, and I was able to see what a thrill it was whenever Johnny advanced in any way. When this took place, it was a great thing in our lives.

Johnny was a wonderful baby. The advantages of syndrome children are that they are sweet and kind and loving, and we have really reaped the rewards of it.

As parents, we get onto what it's like raising children and seeing them go through the same type of development. But it has been different with Johnny, and has actually been exciting to go through these new experiences with him. That has been one of the benefits of having him.

Johnny is patient and long-suffering. Where most babies will scream for their dinner, little Johnny would just patiently wait for Mom to feed him. I had to consciously be aware that I must not wait for the crying, but feed him before he demanded it, because he would just wilt down and go back to sleep, rather than make a fuss. We try not to take advantage of his patience.

Since Johnny's birth we have received much help from different people, giving us a good understanding of the potential of these children. We realized that it is greater than we had ever imagined. Their future is not hopeless and black. With proper stimulation and help they can learn to walk and talk and be trained in their toilet and other personal habits. Even in some situations they can accept certain kinds of jobs and make a livelihood. This helped us to get a better grasp on what our situation would be with Johnny, and also gave me motivation to help him, and to learn how mothers can teach these children. I am a firm believer that from the very first moment of their lives they are starting to learn.

Right from the first day that we told our children about Johnny, we laid the foundation for his progress by explaining that this child is very precious because he has a special spirit, loved by his Father in Heaven. When this life ends for him he will have earned a marvelous reward, a reward that all of us work for and hope to gain. We know that it is guaranteed for Johnny, because of his situation in this life, and it will be well worth it.

This has been a definite influence on our attitudes about Johnny, an important, integral part of our feelings toward him. We feel that he is an asset in our home because he brings so much love and kindness to us.

Johnny is now three years old. We take him to a school for retarded children, where they work with him and tell us of the different stages that we need to help Johnny with. There are certain fundamentals that he needs to learn. He has a very relaxed muscle tone, and he could stand easier than he could crawl. We tried to get him to walk, but they told us, "Forget the walking for now, this boy needs to crawl first." We worked with him for a couple of months, and soon he was scooting around the floor on his hands and knees. Then he was up on his feet and walking. He's also starting to say words, and he communicates well without them, but they tell us to insist that he try to make the sound, and never to respond to his pantomimes and gestures. He must try and communicate vocally, as this gives him the desire to continue to learn.

One day there was a special program at the school, and some of our children took Johnny to it. They had a marvelous time playing with him. I didn't realize the impact that their attention to him had on others until one mother said, "When you see how his brothers treat Johnny, you know why he is so sweet and cute."

The children play with him, read him stories, swing him, wrestle with him. All this gives him stimulation and helps him a great deal.

For our whole family group, especially our children, having Johnny has been one of the greatest experiences that we could ever have. Now that we are over the hump and have finally adjusted to it, we see why it is the will of our Heavenly Father for Johnny to be retarded and to be in our home. We are all here to gain experiences. What a marvelous experience we have gained from having this special child in our home.

My whole feeling toward handicapped children has changed. I can accept them now and understand them better. I have feelings of love toward them, which have replaced feelings of fear, worry and anxiety. These feelings have spread throughout our family. It must have touched sixty or seventy people, not counting all our neighbors, who have just thrown their arms around little Johnny and treated him as though he were a prince. What a marvelous effect this can have on a person's life.

Johnny's future is still uncertain. His father, especially, has a strong desire to work toward the goal of developing Johnny's potential enough so that he can work, rather than just sit around and be bored. This is one of the things that we hope for. Whether or not he will ever have to be institutionalized, we just don't know at this time, we will have to see what seems best. We will continue to love him, to care for him, to work with him and help him in any way we can, and whatever happens we will just have to take it as it comes.

SPECIAL CHILD

Dear Little One—the Father must have known
We had a special need for such as you;
A depth of love unsounded. Unbeknown—
So fathomless a depth before we knew
You, Little One, in whose small hand I see
The hand of childhood, leading, guiding me
Where childhood leads,
Asking no more of life than just *To Be.*

O Beauteous Spirit—caught in this soft clay—
Superimposed with earth for life's short day—
Formed in the shape of love—
Be not over-free
To quit this pleasant prison.
Eternity throughout eternity
Forever beauteous—forever free!

I am content
That you have chosen me.

—Ora Pate Stewart

*B*eatrice Kingsley is a remarkable woman! Our acquaintance with her began with a letter to the editor in a local newspaper. This letter described Bea with words such as compassion, contributed, admired, unselfish, teacher. The friend from a distant state wrote the letter because, in her words, "I thought she shouldn't go unnoticed."

And so she shouldn't. Bea was born in Wyoming, raised in Nebraska, and spent her early married life in Kansas. Her second son was born with cerebral palsy, and so began Bea's struggle to better the world of the child with a defect. Her first attempt was the establishement of a day school for handicapped children in New Mexico. Her husband experienced a heart attack and passed away shortly after this, but Bea pushed on. She attended four different colleges and universities (Eastern New Mexico University, Highlands University, Kearnay State College and Hastings College) to seek training in speech therapy, and continued to work with defective children.

Most recently Bea has been working in a training center of the Institute of Neurological Development in Orem, Utah. Her son and a foster daughter, both severely handicapped, live with her and progress under her expert care. Beatrice Kingsley's life is a beautiful example of true Christian love.

K.J.K.

Chapter 9

My Experience Has Taught Me

By Beatrice Kingsley

"Do something, and if it works, do it some more; if it doesn't work, try something else."

—Franklin D. Roosevelt

When I was a young woman, I remember seeing a small "spastic" boy In a wheelchair being pushed by his mother. How drawn his little arms were and how his face contorted as he tried to speak. I thought, why does she take him out in public? My, how I have remembered those impatient thoughts in the passing years, because I know that many people are thinking the same thoughts when I pass by with my own son in his wheelchair. Although I feel he is a rather handsome fellow, I know that many who are not acquainted with the cerebral palsied do not agree with me.

My son, Dennis, arrived in this world seven weeks premature. He was a two-pounder and the doctor didn't give us much hope for his survival. He was born the day before the attack on Pearl Harbor. My father said that was why he was premature, he wanted to get here while there was a little peace left in the world. He was kept in a twin incubator until he was five weeks old. Then a pair of twin girls were born and he was "kicked out" of his incubator and put into a bed with hot water bottles. He says he's been having girl problems ever since.

When he was nine days old Dennis developed yellow jaundice, caused from an underdeveloped liver. This was the cause of his brain injury. Now it is treated with lights and brain damage seldom occurs.

Dennis did not develop normally. He didn't hold up his head until he was around thirteen months old. He has never sat alone and still uses the arms of his chair for balance. At first we thought of him as being slow because he was premature. His doctor was drafted when Dennis was just past two months old and I never saw him again. I'm sure he could have helped us a lot if he had been available. I got along without a doctor until Dennis was about five months old. Then he developed a bad case of pink eye and it was necessary for us to hunt up another doctor. Dennis was our second child, so I had had some experience with child rearing, but there was yet much for me to learn.

We took him to a specialist when he was about sixteen months old, but in those days they did nothing for him until he was four years old. We were living in northern Oklahoma and we were referred to a specialist in Oklahoma City. The treatment consisted of operations and exercise. At one time Dennis was able to walk with a weighted grocery basket for support, but another operation and a year in casts put him so far back that he was never able to walk again.

A few years ago I heard of a "new" treatment for the brain injured which consisted of teaching the person to crawl and creep as a baby does, in order to retrain the brain. Instead of operations, exercises coordinating the movement of the arms, legs and head into a crawling pattern is done for the person who cannot do it for himself, or is doing it incorrectly. I wish I could tell you that through this treatment Dennis is now going on his own. I can tell you that he was 23 when we started and his knee caps were "frozen" from being in casts so long and had to be "broken" so that they would work again. I can tell you that for the first time in his life he can move his legs a few inches when on his stomach. He will tell you that his head knew his feet were there but his feet didn't know his head was there. I can tell you that his one eye was 20/80 and that now it is 20/40. I can tell you that he sits much straighter and at times can lift his feet. He is still working very hard to gain control of his body. Others with which we work have come much further, but Dennis' age is against him. There is still hope for him, but he must first undo much before he can do what is necessary.

At first I was very optimistic that Dennis would outgrow his problems. I would like to save others from making this same mistake. As the years passed, I began to realize that he would not outgrow them, but would need a lot of help, and I did not think of giving up. Our worst mistake was, and perhaps still is, doing too much for him. Dennis was the type of child who moved very little. The diagnosis was non-tension athetoid. It was so much easier to do things for him than to get him to try to do it for himself. Even yet he will sit in one spot for hours if no one makes him move. In fairness to him, I must say that in the years from about three to nine he did try more, but then as he couldn't seem to make it work, he seemed to give up. This is true of many like him.

His father and grandfather built him many pieces of exercise equipment to help him. He had boxes to support him while sitting, and bars to support him while walking. We were always trying to get him to walk instead of crawl, as we lived in a part of the country where there were a lot of scorpions and I refused to put him on the floor. When he did get on the floor he would pull along with his arms and did not know how to pull to his feet. Another mistake I made was to put him in an infant seat that was too low for him and he developed "back knees" which have caused him a great deal of trouble. How important it is to have the handicapped child around those who have had training and can recognize the danger signals.

We lived too far from centers for children like Dennis, but when he was eleven we lived in New Mexico and a summer camp program was started. I took him there and was surprised at how many children there were who were not in any kind of school program. I decided to start a "school," with some of the other mothers. Later a program was intiated called "Special Education" and Dennis was accepted in this program. It was only held half days, and we decided to keep our "school" for the homebound. With the help of the Elks Lodge and volunteers from the community we were successful. The center is still in operation today.

After Dennis' father died, I decided to return to my mother's home in Nebraska, and it was there that we found the patterning therapy and our life style was changed. We met many wonderful people who came to help. It was through the knowledge and efforts of Mr. Charles Buhrns of Philadelphia that Dennis gained the ability to move his legs.

What advice can I give to the parents of the handicapped children? First, *do not despair!* There is much that can be done to help. Next, treat your child as you would a normal child, within reason. *Expect* from him or her, as you would expect from a normal child, some progress. If he does not notice movement around him by the time he is a few weeks old give him extra stimulation. An activity bar of toys that hangs over the crib—soft toys that make a noise—colored lights that flash—wind chimes—musical toys—mobiles—these will give stimulation. Keep these items around where the child spends his time, and change them often. Play with him and the toys to increase his attention. Older children can be stimulated with tape recorders, stories or records and children's programs on television. Encourage hand and eye play to build coordination. Help the child's eyes to focus by bringing toys close to his face and then taking them a foot or so away and then returning them to within an inch of his nose.

Encourage the child to hold things. Give him a soft toy to sleep with or when spending time on the bed or floor. *Keep the child on his stomach as much as possible.* This strengthens the neck muscles and helps hold up the head. The child should be encouraged to pull his legs up under him as in a swimming motion. Turn the head to the left when laying on his stomach one time and turn it to the right the next time. Alternating each time will help to develop the eyes equally and help to avoid the one-eyed problem so many children have these days. The sleeping pattern to use is to put up the left hand and bend the left leg and turn the head to the left, leaving the right leg and the right arm straight down. This position is used one night and then reversed the next. This can also be used during nap times, especially if cords are tight.

Walking Too Early

I cannot emphasize enough the importance of leaving the child on his stomach for a sufficient period of time. I have seen parents hold a two or three month old child on its feet and encourage it to walk. There seems to be a status symbol about getting your child to walk early. This practice and putting a child in a small play pen curtails the child's activity and puts him on his feet too soon. *The mental processes will be limited because the physical pathways of the brain are not fully developed.* I remember when my first grandchild was crawling. She was almost fourteen months old and everyone including the other grandparents thought my son and his wife were cruel in not helping the child to pull up and try to walk. One day when she was crawling on the lawn she just raised up on her feet and started walking. She never fell down, she never needed to hang on to anything to get up from sitting on the floor. She has been an A student in all her grades in school.

Limiting the crawling can be dangerous. It can turn out "one-eyed" slow readers or those who have trouble with mathmatics. Often there is a lack of coordination and a tendency to be accident prone. Not only is crawling on the stomach important, but crawling correctly. Both arms and legs should move in a reciprocal manner and the head turns toward the hand that is up. This is opposite to the sleeping position, as that is a rest position and the crawling pattern is an action one. If one leg or arm does not extend as much as the other, or if the child uses one side more than the other, or if he doesn't turn his head each time an arm is extended, he should be encouraged to do so. Even paralysis in stroke victims can be rehabilitated by this treatment if their general health is good enough. This is the way to retrain the brain. Damaged cells cannot be used but no one uses all their brain cells, and by returning to the practice of babyhood new cells can be activated to take over for those which have been damaged.

I used to tell a story in my lectures. It went like this: "One day Johnny came home from Sunday School and his mother asked him what he had learned. He said, 'Well, the teacher told us about the Israelites, and they came to the Red Sea and needed to get across. So Moses called up the Seabees and had them put up a bridge and then he called the Air Force to come and bomb it so the Egyptians couldn't get across.' His mother said, 'That wasn't the way your teacher told it, was it?' 'No,' said Johnny, 'But you wouldn't believe the one she told either.'" Then I would say, "Until a miracle like the crossing of the Red Sea comes along, we had best put our shoulder to the wheel." Now I am saying that the miracle has come, but it involves a lot of hard work. I have seen it work.

Operations vs. Exercise

There are many times when operations are necessary, as with the hair lip or hydrocephlic. Many birth defects need surgery, but surgery is not the answer for the brain injured. Have you heard of the town at the foot of the mountain that had a meeting to see what should be done to stop the accidents where cars would fall off the treacherous mountain highway and fall into the town below? The discussion brought out that they could either put a fence at the top of the mountain along the danger spots or they could put an ambulance at the town below to carry the injured and dead. An operation for the brain-damaged is putting an ambulance in the town below. Many are the cases I have seen that regressed through the treatment of casts, braces and operations. Following the normal patterns of babyhood is nature's way, and although a great deal of work is involved it is the only way to a normal life for the brain injured, whether that injury is from birth, accident or stroke. Sometimes when a person does not exercise enough the cords in the body do not grow properly and it is a popular method to operate to lengthen them, but so much is lost through the time in casts and recuperating that it is far better to exercise and rub them with lanolin or similar oils.

Crippled Personality

Crutches are more than the metal or wooden sticks we see. They can be personality crutches. I remember one time my son and I were traveling on the bus from Utah to Texas and several people came by him and put candy and money in his lap. I didn't think much of it until he said, "Mother, that lady didn't give me anything." Then I realized that he was beginning to expect these things and we had a long talk on the subject. The person who relies on his condition hurts himself more than the original injury. A spoiled child is never a happy child. I do not mean that it is good to completely ignore his situation. The new helps for the handicapped, like special parking, lunch privileges and the like are great advantages and should be used.

Discipline

This is a very important part of the treatment of a handicapped child. For the autistic child it is the difference between a life of meaning and a bare existence. Discipline must be unwavering, always the same for the same act. A child needs to know what is expected behavior and what are the rewards and punishments, and it should be administered with love and not anger. A wrong act needs to be corrected at the time of the act and not postponed "until Father gets home." Biting, kicking, screaming is not accepted behavior and to improve, it must be eliminated. *Remember always to do it with love.*

Perhaps the most important thing in the life of a handicapped person is to be treated as normal as possible—in the
attitude of those around them, in taking part in families and
experiences. Dennis' father believed in giving him experiences
which he could not get for himself. He took him up on the roof of
a house and let him look down the chimney. He took him up on
an oil rig where he was working so he could see the countryside.
He took him to the bottom of the big Carlsbad Caverns in New
Mexico, and put him on the back of a pony. He was always included in family outings. These children need not only go, but
they need to have things emphasized to them—the smell of bread
baking, a sudden summer shower, the colors of a hummingbird,
the smell of the pines, the feel of textures, the softness of a rose
petal and the protection from its thorn, the feel of the wind in his
hair and the rain on his face. Everyday things that we take so
much for granted should be called to his attention. Let him sift
the sand through his fingers and most of all hug him and kiss him
and let him know he is loved, and mean it. Give your child the
best, give him your time.

Hydrocephalic or Waterhead

This condition occurs when there is a disturbance in the
system that causes the water in the system to collect in the head
instead of normally leaving the body. This causes the head to
grow to two or three times the normal size and the pressure from
this will cause death. It is now possible for the surgeon to put in
what is called a "shunt" which regulates the condition and elimi-
nates the water. Not having it done is cruel and inhumane. We
must get these children to doctors immediately.

Hair Lip—Cleft Palate

My heart goes out to the parents of a child born with the
severe cleft in the lip. This is a severe shock to the parents and
one which cannot be disguised. Thank goodness it is repairable.
Many competent surgeons are available who can remedy the
problem. It is the early years when impressions are made and a
wise parent will help the child to adjust to the looks and comments of others. Hiding the child will not solve the problem. I've
often reminded my son that it is his mission on earth to educate

others about the handicapped. Perhaps this is the mission of the parents of a child who has this problem.

Mentally Retarded

Much can be done for these children by supervising their early physical development. It is extremely important for these children to follow the normal pattern of babyhood—first learning to roll over, then holding up their heads, pulling along on their stomach and then getting up on hands and knees and creeping. Not only should this be followed exactly, but no incorrect procedures should be allowed. Often this type of child will completely pass by one of these developments and this will result in problems later on. Late walking for the retarded child is good, for the earlier patterns need to be well founded before walking is introduced.

The Under-Achiever

This is the student in school who has trouble keeping up. Often he seems to be above average in many things and is easily discouraged. This is the type of child who gains the most under a supervised program of exercise. Often a few weeks can make the difference. I knew of a child who was having trouble reading and she was brought to me. I asked her to get down on the mat and crawl for me. She was putting up the arm and leg on the same side. I showed her how to cross over to put the opposite arm up and it took her just two days to master it. A summer of work and her patterns were established and her problem was solved. A few weeks and a little training can make the difference between winning and losing.

The Autistic Child

This is the child who lives in a dream world. It is usually caused by brain injury. A crippled child who becomes bored with the world around him can slip into a make-believe world. In extreme cases they can become blind, deaf and unable to move by refusing to cooperate with the physical world around them. An article which appeared in *The Reader's Digest* (April, 1976) entitled *"For the Love of Ann"* is one of the best articles to date. It is the story of an autistic girl and how her parents rehabilitated her and helped her to live a normal life.

Case Histories

I am now working with an autistic child. She is also crippled. She fell off the bed when four months of age and struck her head, piercing the fontanelle (soft spot) with so minimal a break that it went undiscovered for days. Then severe seizures started and she was rushed to a hospital. Although the doctors operated and removed what blood they could, the damage was already done. She was taken to many doctors but none gave her parents any hope. Eventually she was brought to me and through extensive exercising, patience, perseverance, and discipline she has learned to hold a spoon and feed herself. She can move her paralyzed arm and has started to use it as a helping hand. The prognosis—she should continue to improve both mentally and physically until she can lead a fruitful life.

I am also working with an eight-year-old girl who was born with problems caused by formaldehyde poisoning from her mother working during her pregnancy in a plant where formaldehyde was used. The child was unable to tolerate milk of any kind and was put on a mixture of coconut milk and carrot juice. She had many problems with coordination and especially with her eyes. She was unable to keep up in school. After nine months of intensive exercises she is reading first grade material, can do addition and subtraction, her eyes are focusing and she has lost her vacant look. Her mother is proud of the fact that the child has learned to blow her nose and has quit wetting the bed, two problems which have given her much concern.

Clyde was bumped by a car when three years old. There seemed to be no damage at the time, but when he started school, he just couldn't keep up with his class. I put him on the floor and he couldn't crawl. During that summer he learned to crawl. He quickly caught up with his grade and had little trouble keeping up. In fact, he was one of the better students of his class.

Blessings Unawares

I have been asked, "Has having a handicapped child been a blessing, a curse, a limitation?" I am reminded of the words of the patriarch who said, "And you will have blessings unawares." My life, I am sure, is much different than it would have been if my son had been normal. I wonder if I would ever have recognized the great needs of those of the handicapped world. Perhaps, for I have always been a compassionate person. I'm sure I would have found some way to satisfy my need to be needed. But I can say most truthfully that I am glad I was introduced into the world of the handicapped. I'm not happy that my son had to go through his painful experiences of operations and rehabilitation to regain what inactivity had done to him. I'm sorry that he has not had the chance to live a full and normal life. He has wished he could have a wife and a home and family, but he has been unable to, as yet. These things I would like to change. But there are blessings unaware. My health has been better than most people my age; I haven't had time to worry about aches and pains. My back has remained strong and I can lift much more than my peers. I have increased in patience, wisdom and love beyond the expectations of my youth, and I have been rewarded with the love and honor of many fine people with whom I have associated through the years. I would not change my "load" for any I have seen, but my deep regret is for the "load" my son and other handicapped people must bear.

To the parents of these special children I want to say: Love them, talk to them, make them a part of your family. Give them experiences, and remember always that parenthood is a partnership with God and He will help you if you will ask Him.

Section Two

The Handicapped Speak

Greatness is not reached
In one transcendent step—
Nor is it all the same
With one man or another;
We each become, to some degree,
Great in our own way.
In facing grief or pain,
Our extraordinariness
Comes through,
At times surpassing all,
And towering above
The common every-day.

—Sherrie Hundley

*M*ike Johnson is no ordinary person. About ten years ago he joined the U. S. Marines and volunteered to fight at the front in the Vietnam war. When he returned home, his legs and part of his hands were missing, but this situation has not kept Mike from doing the things he wanted to do in life. With his built-in determination and energetic outlook, he was able to overcome the many frightening obstacles which faced him. It was difficult. Mike fought the despondency and useless feelings which come with such a loss. Through prayer and the help of his family, he recovered from his injuries and returned to college where he met and married a lovely girl from Orem, Utah. They are working hard to maintain their home in Alpine and to raise a family.

Mike has participated in many athletic events for wheelchair victims. At the World Olympics for the Physically Disabled in Toronto, Canada he was the recipient of two gold medals, one silver and one bronze medal, having the distinction of being top athlete on the United States team for the physically disabled.

He is active in church organizations and has coached young men in basketball competition, where they have won top honors in stake and regional events.

How has Mike done it? In his own words, "I am not a quitter!" He has no legs, but he has something that many of us do not have—the ability to get up again and again when life literally knocks him off his feet. He does it by setting goals—and then working very hard to reach them.

S.A.H.

Chapter 10

Get On With the Business of Living

By Mike Johnson

"Nothing in the world can take the place of persistence."
—*Calvin Coolidge*

In 1965 I left my West Virginia home and travelled to Utah to attend Brigham Young University. The first year I didn't do much in school, preferring to spend my time mountain climbing and enjoying the out-of-doors. At that time the Vietnam war was at its peak, and, after reading a book called The Green Beret, I became all jazzed up about wanting to go and fight. My father had been a marine and I wanted to be with what I considered the best outfit, so I talked to a marine recruiter. I thought I was going just to talk, but when I had been there about fifteen minutes, I had signed up. I was a marine!

I had some time until I had to report, so I went home to tell my parents I had joined the marines. I think they were a little disappointed.

In February, 1967 I was stationed at Camp Pendleton, where I completed basic training in jungle warfare and combat fighting.

I was shipped to Vietnam in June and found myself near Danang, which is in the northern part of what was then South Vietnam. I was to be with communications, then machine gunnery, and then, when things got hot, they needed guys in the infantry. I wanted to get out where the fighting was. They thought I was nuts, but they sent me out. I thought all my friends would come out and join me, but they stayed back in battalion and took clerk jobs.

About six months after I had gone out I had my 20th birthday. My company moved southwest of Danang where the enemy had better control of the area. We had to go out on search-and-destroy missions, and were losing a man a day.

On January 29, 1968, we were running a mission in a village and we got a call on the radio to go back to the landing zone. A helicopter was going to pick us up and take us back to AnHoa where the air base was located. Then we would walk from there to our base as road security for a mine-sweeping team. We spent the night in AnHoa, sleeping inside and having good, hot meals for the first time in ages. The next morning we started marching back toward our base. The engineers were sweeping the roads for mines and we were acting as security at the sides of the road. My squad was on the left side and another squad was on the right. We'd walked a few hours when suddenly one of the guys a couple of yards away hit a booby trap by a tree and was blown backwards. He wasn't hurt too badly, but they brought a truck to take him back to the base.

We then spread our men way out, knowing that the place was booby trapped. I was walking down a kind of small incline covered with tangled vines and deep grass. It was impossible to see any kind of trip-wire. I was thinking this would be a good place for a booby trap, and the next thing I knew I was in the air. I don't remember hearing the explosion, but I came down in the big hole that it made, and I do remember the burning, the dirt, the smell. I remember seeing my left leg gone and my right leg bent the wrong way. I remember saying, "Doc, it hurts," yet I don't actually remember the pain. It didn't really register when I saw that my leg was gone. I was conscious and I remember the radioman was calling them to come and get me. The squad leader and lieutenant were leaning over me, trying to get me to say the Lord's prayer. I guess they thought I was going to die. I couldn't even remember the Lord's prayer, and I thought to myself, "Brother, you've had it now. If you can't remember the Lord's prayer, where is He going to be now that you need Him?" Someone said it and I repeated it for a little ways, and then I passed out.

I don't remember the helicopter ride back to Danang. I woke up in the hospital with tubes coming out of my arms, my chest and my neck. I do remember the white sheets, the nurses and the bright lights, but I still don't remember the pain, only flashes of coming to and knowing where I was. I had been there before when I had malaria, so I knew I was in the hospital. The doctors talked over me, and then I was wheeled in for operations. My left leg had been blown off, and the right one was shattered. They later had to amputate it just above the knee.

I remember one night when they were working on my left hand, with a big bright light over my bed. We started getting hit outside. I could hear the explosions, lots of yelling, shouting, screaming, and shooting. They were evacuating the guys from the hospital, but I couldn't be moved, so they put me under the bed and put a mattress over me. A nurse with a helmet on gave me a shot and said, "That's all I can do for you."

When I woke up I was in a plane headed for what I assumed to be the States, but they were taking me to the Philippines. We had to make an emergency stop in Japan because my right leg had burst open and they found me in a pool of blood. My heart was beating at some ridiculous figure, trying to pump what blood was left. I knew then that I was close to dying, but things still seemed rather vague—not really true. In Japan they operated and sewed the leg with stainless steel wire, but that night it broke open again and the operation had to be done all over again. That is the most pain I remember. It was excruciating. They put a blood pressure cuff on me and pumped it up like a tourniquet. I was screaming and yelling with pain. They put me back on the plane and took me to the Philippines where I spent about seven days. There I was able to call my parents, and I told my Dad, "Don't worry, I'm not too bad. I've just lost my legs—nothing really serious." Dad thought I had lost my brains, too. They had been told not to expect me to live because there was so much damage, but when he heard me talk, he said that he knew I was going to make it, so he threw a big pizza party at home.

In the Philippines they told me that I had all my fingers, and that made me feel better. That had been one of my biggest worries. I was all bandaged up and couldn't see anything. One eye had been operated on. I couldn't hear very well because my eardrums had been broken. When I got to Bethesda Naval Hospital, they said to me, "Now, it's going to be a shock for you when you see your hands." Then they took the bandages off and I'll never forget how I felt. I was missing a thumb and two fingers on my left hand and my other two fingers were really beat up. I had a huge slice out of my forearm and the right hand was just as bad as the left. Both were absolutely butchered. It made me sick, and I was furious that they had told me my fingers were there! How could they have done that to me?

I thought I could never live with this. It seemed almost worse than losing my legs. What could I ever do without good hands? I had feelings of great despair and was deeply puzzled about what I would do with my life. I wondered how I could ever marry, and my attitude became very negative. I knew that I would never be the same again, with my legs and part of my hands gone. I would have to spend the rest of my life as a different kind of man—a disabled man.

Then, slowly, I began to realize that it is not what you have, but what you do with what you have that counts in your life. I knew there was no need to feel bitter or cheated, because it was of my own choice that I had gone to fight. It was no one's fault that I had been on top of that booby trap when it went off, even though another man later wrote me and said that he was the one who had tripped the wire. I knew the risks I was taking when I went, but I wanted to go and fight. I may have killed or injured men in battle, too, and didn't know it. I didn't blame my country or anyone. It was just one of those things and you have to learn to live with it. When I thought it over, I could see that they were right in telling me I had my fingers. When I got back to the States and was in a little better shape, I was better able to cope with it. Now I just had to figure out what I was going to do.

I guess my Mom and Dad—my whole family—were responsible for my coming out of it. They were just super. They stayed right with me, worked with me, and Dad was the type of guy who would never let me quit. I know my recovery was due to the caring of my family and an answer to prayers. I had been given several blessings while in the hospital, and it gave me much strength and courage through all my operations and rehabilitation. My testimony of the power of God was really strengthened, and has continued with me ever since. I knew that someday I would get back the limbs I had lost—that it was just in this life that I would have to do without them, and this is a short time, even though it may sometimes seem long.

Slowly I began to change my attitude from what I couldn't do to what I could do, and how well could I do it. It was then that I started coming uphill. Sure, I couldn't help thinking, "I won't be able to drive a car. I can't play football," but I decided that if there were ways to do these things, I would find them. Once I did that,

I started straightening out and I pulled myself out of the hole that I was in and could have stayed in if I wasn't careful.

My greatest struggles in my rehabilitation were not with my physical limitations—not with the changed body. Facing other people seemed to be the toughest of my problems—the people who stared, who were rude, or who had a lot of pity. I didn't handle that very well. I just couldn't accept it when I knew they were saying, "You poor thing," or "That's too bad." Sometimes kids still bother me a little. They say, "How do you walk?" or "Can you feel anything?" or "Do your feet itch?" But I remember when I used to do the same kind of thing when I'd see a guy with a limp or something, and so I know they're just inquisitive. When they ask me what happened, I just tell them I got hit by a train, so they had better watch out for trains.

Rehabilitation didn't come all at once. It took a long time to get used to getting in and out of my wheelchair, and learning to do many things all over again. You have to experiment. I think that's the way it should be. There was no one in the hospital to show me how to do things, I just had to figure it out by myself. That's the way it would be, and if I had it to do over again, that's the way I'd want it. I wouldn't want someone telling me, "Okay, now you can get out of bed," and "now you can take your shower," or "you can go down the stairs. You do it this way." Maybe there's some people who would need help, but in my case it was good that I had to learn it on my own. It was really good for me. It has taken a long time, but I was determined to do it. I have even learned to play basketball, to run track, and many other things, but it took a lot of work and a long time. My whole family is athletic and I had always enjoyed athletics in high school. I was determined that I was not going to give them up, so when I got back to my home in West Virginia, I played ball with my brothers in the back yard.

Since then I have been doing a lot in the way of athletics. Most people are very surprised. They can't believe that I can "run" six miles a day or that I can do a hundred yard dash in so much time. They see me going around in the fields and they say, "gee, you shouldn't be doing that." They seem to have their stereotypes set about people in wheelchairs, and some even say, "I wonder why he doesn't just quit." But most people are pretty good. People that are the same age as Jan and I accept us as a couple just like anybody else.

Jan is my wife, and we have a son about a year old. My first and greatest goal is to make my home the happiest place I can possibly make it, and that is what I'm working for.

My disablement has brought many blessings in my life. I know it has really helped me to grow. I know that I care more about other people than I used to. I have worked at the State Hospital and I have found that I have a kind of inner feeling about people and when there is something wrong. I didn't have that before. I know it is true what they say about people who have lost their ability in one area becoming stronger in some other area. It hasn't made me any smarter, but I enjoy what I get from learning, and I hope that someday I can put it to good use and help others. I am hoping to be a basketball coach and health teacher someday.

Several years ago we started a team in Salt Lake called the Rimriders. It has been a great challenge and I have tried to make myself the best in the country. It has become more than just a desire to go out and compete, it's to go out and win. With me it's a matter of being the best of whatever I can be. I have competed in meets in Colorado, California and New York, and later went to California where there were about 1300 individuals from 52 countries taking part in the World Wheelchair Olympics. I felt it a great honor to be chosen for the Olympic team.

Looking back now on all that has happened to me, I guess I would have to say that the worst part of it was the discouragement that hit me when I first realized that I was handicapped. I don't like that word "handicapped"—it seems to put such a negative aspect to the thing. A better word might be "Disabled"—although I don't really like that either. It seems to tell you that a guy has got something wrong but he's not necessarily limited in what he can do. Actually I don't think of myself as either, I just think of myself as another guy.

There is only one way to face being handicapped or disabled and that is to pull your head out and get on with the business of making your life as normal as possible. I didn't like being treated different or special. Sometimes with a handicapped person it takes extra amounts of love, and those who are closely associated with him must be extra sensitive to his needs or his feelings. Treat him as normal as possible, and know when you are pushing too far. It is difficult to know how much to do for a person and how much to let him do for himself. If he has the mentality for it, then you should put the pressure on and say, "Okay, now you have two choices. You can either sit on your can and do nothing or you can get out and make something of your life!"

When I would get really down I'm sure my Dad wanted to say, "It's all right, son, you just sit back and relax..." but that's not the way to do it. You tend to slip into a pit, feeling sorry for yourself, and if you do that too many times, you're going to fall in and stay in. Despair is like a narcotic, it gets harder and harder to get rid of as you go along.

One of the greatest things in my life is that Jan and I can laugh at our problem. One night we were watching a movie with John Wayne, in which he lost his leg. It was a real serious matter, this losing a leg, but I found myself asking, "How will he walk? Does his foot itch?" and we were really cracking up. I find I can face things much better if I have a sense of humor about it and not take it too seriously. Sometimes my friends carry it to extremes with jokes about me, like saying I haven't a leg to stand on, but most of the time they're real good to me. I hunt and fish with them and we have great times. They treat me just like anybody else, and that's great!

Maybe sometimes I'm too light-hearted about it, but it helps to keep me from thinking about my troubles and falling back into that pit. I have to keep going, and I know that when I get my legs back in the next life, I'm going to burn up the ground with 'em!

I know I've come a long way, with God's help. Maybe someday I'll be able to help someone do the same.

*L*orna Simper is a victim of cerebral palsy. When she was a small child, her parents faced the decision of whether or not to place her in an institution or raise her at home. It was their decision to keep her at home with the rest of their large family. Lorna feels that being raised with many brothers and sisters was a great asset to her. She says her parents didn't have time to spoil her or pamper her, even though they did have to spend many hours nursing her through illnesses, operations, bruises and stitches. Through their loving persistence and patience and from her father teaching her to laugh at her own clumsiness, Lorna has learned to look at life as a beautiful experience.

In her story, Lorna shares many ideas and feelings about what parents can do to help in the raising of a child with special problems. She lets you know that there are always two sides to a handicap—the side that makes you cry and the side which can make you laugh. Whichever you do most, is all up to you.

K.J.K.

Chapter 11

Only in the Eyes of Man

By Lorna Simper

"The great pleasure in life is doing what people say you cannot do." —*Walter Bagehot*

Pardon me for intruding right now but maybe I can help. I know that you have had a terrible shock and that it's going to take some time to get used to the fact that your baby is going to be handicapped. Right now that's an awful lot for your mind to grasp. Maybe I can help make all of that a little palatable. I have cerebral palsy and I know the kind of thing that you're going through.

If you're like a lot of parents, I would imagine that you have some guilt feelings to contend with. These feelings are normal, but be assured that they aren't justifiable. The causes of cerebral palsy are many and varied, some of them known and some of them unknown. Since all the causes are not clearly identified, there are too many variables to nominate yourself or your partner for permanent scapegoat duty. Realize that as a wise man once said: "Placing blame is the providence of God and small children." Let your mind be at ease—God isn't punishing you, your mate or your baby. Remember the Bible story of the blind man. When the apostles asked Christ who had sinned to cause his blindness, his parents or the man? The Savior answered them that no one had, but that the man was blind to show the power of God. If you will let your child, he can teach you many things about the Almighty and His love.

Going hand in hand with guilt feelings are extreme fears about the future. You're going to have to learn how to walk tall in a crowd and look past the giggles, and the pity, and the scorn of the ignorant. Your child's handicap is only a negative reflection on you if you let it become such. When hard situations come up, just remember that small comments come from people with small minds. One of the things that is paramount in your child's acceptance of himself is the feeling that his parents not only love him but are not ashamed of him. Anyway, the thoughts and feelings of other people are their problem that they have to work out for themselves. You can help them change their precast ideas if they want to, but those ideas aren't your responsibility or the responsibility of your child.

I can't allay your financial fears. There are going to be a lot of doctor bills! There's no way around it. Even those financial problems can be something that draws your family together. If the bills become more than you can handle, make use of your immediate family. Go to them and ask for help. If this is an impossibility, make use of the community, state, and national programs set up especially to help defray medical costs. Charity, above all, is defined as pure love. What greater compliment could the community pay your baby than extending that love to you.

School for your baby will probably begin before he or she is two years old. By school I don't necessarily mean reading and writing: The mastering of many motor skills won't be accomplished without some professional help. There are many preschools and nursery schools throughout the country that are especially geared to the needs of the handicapped preschooler. Also, become involved with a physcial therapy program immediately. Most kids can wait until they are five for professional help. Your child can't.

Learn to look past your child's disability and become acquainted with the person that he is. This is not to say that you should submerge the fact that your child is handicapped. Nothing could be more detrimental to both you and your child. Just learn to realize that the person who is your child is much more complex than the mere fact of his palsy. Help your child build on the positive aspect of his life and direct him in the forming of success-oriented goals that are within his ability to accomplish. The achieving of the first set of goals will provide the impetus for higher and higher achievement. The child needs to feel that the whole world is not out of his grasp.

Learn to be mean! That may sound shocking but one of the most important things you can do for your child is to let him skin his knee and then get back up by himself. Insist that he dress himself as much as possible; even if his part in the process takes him half an hour. Give your child as much independence as he can handle, as soon as he is able to handle it. Sometimes your child will need prodding to learn to do things for himself, but the best thing you can do is expect of him as much as he can give. It is very important that, as parents, you expect realistic things of your child. It is not realistic to expect a child confined to a wheelchair with a great many involuntary movements to button small buttons, but in many cases a child who has this much involvement can dress himself in clothes that have no buttons.

There will be times when your child will come in contact with the harsh realities of childhood and he will come to you for answers to the unanswerable "Why?" This is a very important time in your child's life. It is vital that you have settled the question once and for all in your mind, because the answer you give him many affect the rest of his life. The elements of that answer are really knowing your child and having buried your own puzzling over the question. If you, the parent, don't dwell on "Why?", then answering why won't be as hard on either of you.

Teach your child how to live with the world on the world's own terms. Help him work out ways to solve his own frustrations by himself. One of the best ways to do this is to be completely honest with your child concerning his disability. It is much easier if the child knows why his leg shakes rather than sitting and wondering. This honestly should be something that the child grows up with and not something that is suddenly thrust upon him. This can make him feel like a sideshow freak. It is so important that the child grows up knowing that his handicap is part of him, but that it isn't something he should be ashamed of. One of the byproducts of this honesty is that your child will be open and honest with the people around him. It is much easier for a child to answer the question, "Why do you walk funny?" if he knows why he does.

Another way to help your child make peace with the world is to teach him to laugh at life. There are many situations that are really funny if one has the right attitude. I was once asked if my brains rattled when I walked. The person who asked the question was sincere and so she received an honest *no!,* and then we both started to giggle. Teach your child not to take the world or himself too seriously and to be comfortable enough with himself that he can laugh without any qualms, at any funny situation.

Along with teaching your child to live with the world, there'll be times when you may have to strive to teach the world how to live with your child. There could be times when you, the parent, may have to lead the fight to eradicate the barriers that face your child. I am not recommending that any parent should become incensed when life doesn't fall into place exactly as their child may have wished it to fall. I am stating that your handicapped child has just as much right to make his own successes and failures as any other child does, and you, as his parents, must do everything in your power to safeguard that right. Just make sure that, as you fight for his rights, you don't go too far and rob him of the right to fail. It is a great lesson for any person when he learns that failure is not a climax in defeat, but an enlarging of success-ladened horizons. He has the right to learn that failure is not the end of the world and its possibility.

The real key to your child being able to integrate himself into the world around him is how well the child has become an integrated part of the family unit, but *only a part* of the family.

It is easy for many parents to make the handicapped baby the focal point of their whole life at the expense of the rest of the family and all too often at the expense of each other also. A wife must never forget that at times she must be a wife first; there are also times when her child needs discipline more than to be loved or cuddled. The same thing goes for the father. He must not neglect his husbandly responsibilities and he also needs to let his disabled son or daughter know that he loves that child through the use of correction.

When your handicapped child needs and deserves praise, praise him. By the same token, when he needs and deserves discipline, discipline him. Teach your child that the world isn't a "something-for-nothing" place but a place where he must earn and deserve the successes he accomplishes. This is done by teaching him right and wrong; by teaching him that he is important to you because you care about his actions. This is a lesson he will never learn if he is robbed of the gift of correction when he needs it.

If there are other children in the family, involve them in the special care that the handicapped child needs. Make them feel important and it will be easier for them to accept the disabled child. It is easy sometimes to forget that your children who aren't physically disabled have very urgent needs of their own. It is important for both your handicapped and non-handicapped child that the needs of the non-handicapped child are not neglected. Leave your handicapped child with a babysitter and go watch your other children in the school band. You may think that this is excluding the handicapped child from the family circle but there are times when this kind of individualized attention is just what your family needs. It is a hard but valuable lesson for any child when he learns that he isn't the center of the universe and the rest of the family really doesn't revolve around him. This is not saying that every time there is an outing it is advisable to leave your handicapped child home. On the contrary, for every hundred times the family goes out there might be one time that the handicapped child needs to stay home. Parents must be very aware of their own home situation to know when this is needed.

I know that I have been giving a lot of advice and you have every right to wonder what about a real life time situation. How do all those things work without the power of the pen to back them up!

Much of that answer only you and time and perseverance can decide. But let me share a story that might help during the times when you think that nothing will work.

I was born with water on the brain (hydrocephalus) and as a result of the brain damage caused by this condition I was left with ataxic cerebral palsy. When I was nine months old, my parents were told to put me in an institution for the severely retarded because that was going to be my lot. Through many prayers, long talks and a special priesthood blessing, my parents decided that they would keep me in the home. During my first year they nursed me through whooping cough, pneumonia, and two major operations. When I had my first surgery, the insurance company promptly cancelled their policy and my parents had to stand that $1,000 bill by themselves. That may not sound like much but 25 years ago that was a good-sized amount.

My childhood was a long string of bumps and bruises. When I was six years old, I decided that it was time for me to learn to walk down stairs instead of slide down them. I averaged about one trip to the doctor per week to get my head stitched up after unsuccessful attempts. My parents didn't disuade me and I'll never forget how proud they were when I finally mastered the skill. They let me learn to face life on its own ground and were happy with me when I won.

I became well acquainted with the rules in my house at a very, very early age and I also found out what the consequences for disobedience were. I received my fair share of spankings and most of them were rightly deserved.

My parents have always fought for my right to try. In the fourth grade there was a time when my teacher tried to have me forced out of school. My folks worked through proper channels and I was able to complete my education in the regular classroom. (The situation was such that I either stayed in the normal classroom or I was forced out of school completely.)

My father taught me how to laugh at myself and my own clumsiness which has been one of the greatest gifts he has given me. Life is beautiful, especially when you can laugh at it. I have completed three years of college and a full time proselyting mission for my church. The main reason I am succeeding in life is because my parents taught me who I am; a capable important daughter of her Heavenly Father and that if I keep the Lord on my side, nothing is impossible.

My greatest goal in life is to be a special education teacher and to spread some of the good things that I have experienced on to other people who haven't found out that the shape of their tomorrows is whatever they mold it to be.

So don't ever give up. Life has too many good things in store for you and your child. There is something that your child can do better than any other child in the world. All you have to do is help him focus in on that something and watch him achieve.

GOD GRANTED ME A STUMBLE

When I set out on life's large task,
   God granted me a stumble
     that I might walk, my hand in His;
The beauty of working for words,
   to know the joy of speaking heart to heart.
He gave me sickness
   that I might taste the honey of being robust.
He taught me to trust tomorrow
   and in that trust to find immeasurable success.
He ordained me to match life's little things,
   thereby to see myself and others as Deity's offspring.
I count these blessings precious
   though the world won't understand.
The only place I hobble
   is in the eyes of man.

                            Lorna Simper

Margaret is an inspiration to know. She was born in 1949 in Salt Lake City and raised in Grantsville, Utah. During her pre-natal development some genetic factors malfunctioned which caused birth defects. Her legs between the hip and the knee are missing, she has one shrunken arm permanently bent and the other developed only to the elbow.

From early childhood Margaret has accomplished what peo-ple said she could never do. Going to elementary and high school for her education was a challenge, but she graduated in 1968 from Grantsville High School. A year was spent at Dixie College, and then she went on to Brigham Young University where she gradu-ated in Latin in 1976. People said that her giving missionary service for her church was impossible, but Margaret served a very successful mission in North Texas.

Margaret now works for the Genealogical Department of the LDS Church in Control Extraction. Her interests are wide and she is extremely involved in church-related activities. Margaret's deep testimony of her knowledge that she is a daughter of Father-in-Heaven has affected many.

K.J.K.

Chapter 12

The Challenges of My Life

By Margaret Van Noy

"We need not pray for great opportunities,
but rather the willingness to do little things
in a great way...."

—*Ethel F. Lord*

I was born with birth defects affecting every limb of my body. I am sure that it was a shocking and heartbreaking experience for my parents. I know that the pain they felt at that time far exceeded any pain or grief I would experience during my lifetime.

The doctors said that I would not live and when I lived they said I would be bedridden and never move. When I jumped out of bed and crawled and moved, they said I would never go to school, lead a normal life, or accomplish any of those things which the physically "whole" accomplish. They were wrong, and even now at 25 years of age and having gone to high school, served a mission for the LDS Church, and graduated from college, I still have to convince people that I am a successful, productive, active, functioning human being with a great deal to offer the world!

My early childhood, as far as I can remember, was a fairly active and happy one. I had friends on the block with whom I played the normal games that children play. My mother *never* hovered over me, protecting me like an overly-worried hen. When

I reached the age of six years, my parents did not think I would be able to go to school all day, so my mother took me to school each day after the other kids went home so that the first grade teacher could teach me to read and write. After several weeks the teacher decided that I would go to school as a regular student. By the way, an administrative assistant told the teacher that she was wasting her time trying to do anything with me; but she was certain I could attend. So my father made a cart and put it on wheels so that I could get around. I attended public school until I graduated as a senior. I even served as studentbody vice president my senior year. When I look back on those years, I don't remember ever lacking for friends. There was a period of time, however, when my circumstances depressed me terribly. It was during my 7th and 8th grade years in school. I saw no future for myself. I felt sorry for myself. Then in the 9th grade I had an English teacher from Georgia. She was well educated and I worshipped her. She introduced me to Shakespeare and Dickens who, in turn, introduced me to characters and places I did not know existed. The teacher liked me very much and always told me I had a good, perceptive mind. What a boost to my self-confidence! "Maybe I will go to college," I thought. So, after that I had direction in my life. I did go to college and graduated with a B.A. in Latin.

An education was important to me, but the greatest motivating force in my life was my faith in God. I knew that He loved me and would never let me down. Paul, in the Book of Philippians, said "I can do all things through Christ which strengtheneth me."

At twenty years I decided I wanted to go on a mission for the Mormon Church. "A mission? That's impossible! What could I do?" many people asked. A mission was emotionally and physically taxing. It meant a tremendous amount of walking and knocking on doors. But I knew I could do it. Fortunately, my bishop and my stake president had no doubt that I could serve. As I waited for the calling from the Church leaders, people doubted that I would be accepted. Finally my acceptance papers came. I was going to Texas in the Dallas area. It was a reality. But I had to face more non-believers. The mission president in Salt Lake tried to talk me into going home. When I asked "Do you believe a person could do anything with the help of God?", the answer was no. I felt sorry for him. I served and I knocked on doors, telling people about the gospel. It was a great experience. I never was concerned about the reaction of those people behind the doors I knocked on. If my physical situation had any effect, good or bad, I will never know. My missionary experiences had a very positive effect on my life. After my mission I returned to Brigham Young University.

Finally graduation from college came and I began a full-time job. I have been greatly blessed. In fact, my handicap has been more of a blessing than a burden. There have been many experiences I may not have had otherwise. I believe my life will continue to be successful.

You may be asking yourself, "What things did her parents do to help her?" There were really no special techniques or special thought-out plans used by my parents while I was growing up. All I can tell you is, I was treated normally. That is what you want for your child, isn't it, a normal life? Goethe said, "If you treat a person as he is, he will stay that way, but if you treat him as you want him to be, he will become that." I wish every handicapped child could have the parents I had.

I have seen some cases of handicapped children who, because of the parents' tremendous desire to protect them, have been smothered into total dependence by their parents. I would like to share some of those things to do and not to do so that your child will become as self-sufficient and independent as possible.

First: Treat your child as a normal child. Certainly there are some allowances that have to be made according to the degree of the handicap, but if you use wisdom and do not let selfishness in, you will know what to do.

Second: Don't make excuses for your child. Using a handicap as an excuse for emotional depression or refusal to try things is very dangerous and will lull a person into lethargic security. He will never make the effort to adjust and become independent because he knows he is handicapped.

Third: Give him responsibilities. Everyone needs to feel useful. Feeling useful is very therapeutic for any emotional or physical handicap. Give him things to do around the house. See to it that he does his share of the work. Don't make excuses for him and don't let *him* make excuses. Of course, ability varies, but find *something* to do, even if it is sorting clothes or folding socks. If the handicap is motionless, then give him responsibilities where he would have to use his mind: like planning family outings, deciding on the menu for supper, working up a work load schedule for the other children, or helping make major family decisions. Ask his advice on personal problems, and make him feel useful. When a person cannot function well physically, his mind is going to become twice as active. Read newspapers to him. Discuss politics with him. Help him to channel his thoughts in the right direction. There is nothing more spiritually destructive than to have nothing to think about.

Fourth: Prepare your child for the reaction of the world. It is natural to want to protect him from the staring eyes and criticizing comments of strangers. That is wrong. Your child needs to learn to accept himself and others need to learn to accept him, too. I don't mean display him, but don't hide him. No one ever gets used to being stared at or pointed at. I am not used to it yet. But I do understand it and am able to cope with it. It is human nature for some, unfortunately, to gape at that which they don't understand.

Dating is something I never participated in, but I can honestly say I have not missed it. I have many friends to keep me busy and I have developed interests which keep me happy: church activities and reading (a good book always keeps me cheered). The important thing is to stay happy. I have learned that it is a person's circumstances which make him happy. It comes from within—"As a man thinketh, so is he." I have always had a desperate desire to be happy. That is half the battle, deciding to be happy, and then realizing it does not take a pretty body or a date every weekend. When one is cheerful, he is pleasant to be around and soon deformities or ugliness no longer exist. To a friend, a person's spirit is more vivid than his face. If your child understands this, it will be easier to be amiable. If he can't go outside, then think of ways to entice some of the neighborhood children in for a period of time during the day. If your child is one who is happy and likes himself and others, soon friends will come without enticement. If there are questions asked by these kids about the birth defects, answer them in a relaxed manner. As soon as children's curiosities are satisfied, they cease to concentrate on what they could not understand before.

Fifth: Help your child help himself. Someday you will leave him alone, either because of death or other reasons. Or he may leave you to go to school. Teach him to cook, to sew, to iron. Show him how to use the mass transit system and teach him never to be afraid to ask for help from a stranger. People like knowing they helped out another person. There are many seriously handicapped people who are independent because they have adapted themselves to normal tasks. An example is that for me, walking is difficult. My legs do not have the needed joints to move them independently. I am also missing my right arm to my elbow. So crutches would not have been much help either. My father designed and made a pouch to attach to the crutch which provides leverage so that I could move the crutch. Now I get around fine. I am just a little slow. I have heard of cases in which a woman had no arms at all but she learned to type with a pencil in her mouth. Another woman became so dexterious with her toes that she could do everything with her feet. Anything can be done: it just takes thought, desire, and a little courage to do it.

May I say again, treat a handicapped person normally, and instill in your child this thought: It is not the condition of the body which renders a person disabled but the condition of the mind.

At a Governor's banquet in Salt Lake City, special awards were given to twenty-four citizens of Utah who have overcome the obstacles of being handicapped. Among them was Dennis Dean, a muscular dystrophy victim since the age of six who has been confined to a wheelchair since age twelve. Not only has he overcome problems of his own handicap, but he has been instrumental in helping to develop useful programs for other handicapped people as well.

Now twenty-six years old, Dennis is married, has fulfilled a full-time mission, holds a master's degree in education and hopes to spend his future helping others in the counseling field. This has all been accomplished in spite of the fact that he has had very limited use of his motor muscles.

Though he can move about only with the use of a motorized wheelchair, there is not a doubt that Dennis Dean is really going places.

S.A.H.

Chapter 13

My Chair and I

By Dennis Dean

"Aim at the sun. You may not reach it, but your arrow will fly higher than if you aimed at something on a level with yourself."
                                                    —Joel Hawes

When the doctors diagnosed that I had muscular dystrophy, I felt a kind of despair that I had never known. To my family the news was tragic. We all wondered how such a thing could happen to us. How could we face the challenges which would come? My greatest phobia was what my friends would think of me. Would any of them still be my friends? I wanted to crawl into a shell where no one could see me, yet at the same time I was afraid of being left out and forgotten.

I would sit in the corner of my room and gape at the wheelchair in the opposite corner, where it sat coldly promising confinement and complete restriction to me. Yet the painful struggle of just moving from place to place by myself was increasing day by day.

It was a most difficult adjustment to admit to myself that I was really crippled. I fought with it for some time, and then finally when I could face it in the affirmative—when I could finally say, "Yes, I am physically limited," I was on my way. I found that I was better off with a wheelchair than without one. I could then acknowledge my weaknesses and begin to accentuate my strengths.

After a few months in the wheelchair, I began to realize that it was easier than I had thought it would be. I named my chair Betsy, and she soon became my greatest ally. She helped me to do the things that I could not do alone.

Of course, I had to rely on the help of others. My family soon learned that cooperation was the key to our happiness. Schedules were set up as to who would give me a bath and when, who would get me out of bed, who would pick me up after school. I grew to love each one so much more than I ever could have, had I been able to do all these things on my own.

I once heard it said that nothing is difficult in life, only challenging. When I hear of people who have found themselves in a seemingly tragic situation, such as death in the family or loss of health, etc., I cannot help but smile within myself, for I know that through challenges come opportunity for sacrifice and growth. When these challenges come, it is up to each of us to make a choice as to how we will face it. We can sit and "stare at the wheelchair in the corner," hating the very idea of it, dreading it, refusing to make use of it. Or we can climb into it and make up our mind to let it be our friend and to help us get the most out of life that we possibly can, under the conditions.

There are many people in the world with situations like mine. I would like to say to them that the first thing to do when you find out you have a definite problem is to *take courage!* The initial shock of finding out that something is wrong magnifies the awesomeness of the challenge that lies ahead. I will not try to tell you that it will be easy or that there will not be times of unhappiness and discouragement, but there need not be a complete denial of hope. There can be much good come from the bad.

Next, you must decide what you want to do with your life now that you have a handicap. Analyze the situation and then say to yourself, "What positive things can come from the situation? How can I develop my best potential?"

A very important thing to remember is that mental and physical adjustments go hand in hand. They are a real and necessary problem with which you will have to cope. You must tell yourself that you cannot hide behind your handicap, but that to be able to live life to the fullest, you must realize that you will have to experience effort, sacrifice, hard work and disappointment in order to develop your strengths and enjoy satisfaction from them. When we live with a handicap we must be realistic and yet positive, allowing others to help in the areas with which we need help. And above all, we must learn to be patient! Only with patience and a full awareness of the possibilities can we accomplish what we set out to do.

I owe my life to my family. My parents were faced with the problem of whether to shelter and pamper me or to treat me as an equal with my brothers and sisters. Luckily for me, they chose the latter. I was not shown favoritism but was required to go to school and to do my share of the chores in the home. Of course, I did not do the same things as the others, as I was not able to do hard physical labor, but I could write family letters, help with the finances and keep my area of the house clean. We all learned that the physical things in life are not the most important, but that love of each other and a closeness to God take priority. We learned that a handicap has many blessings, but they do not come all at once.

I worked hard for many years before I learned that my greatest strength was my handicap. Learning to make the best of what we have is a life-long process. Once we have gained one level of independence we are ready for the next. I not only learned to work hard, but to use my mind and to rely on others. I learned that I had more friends than I ever dreamed of, and I have seen many people gain happiness by sacrificing their time and efforts to help me. It has been a great example of putting me first and themselves second.

Most of all I have learned that we are here to do the best with what we have in life, however great or however limited our abilities may be. I have seen the goodness of mankind, and they have gained pleasure by seeing the goodness in themselves.

How grateful I am for my handicap! From my wheelchair I have observed the beauties of God's world, I have enjoyed the blessings of his love and I have realized the greatness in others, as well as the potential in myself. I have also found within myself a kind of inner peace and joy which I might never have known, had I not been handicapped. I want to be able to help others to also find that peace, and to realize that by accepting the "Betsy" in their lives, they can travel the road to happiness—rough as it may seem.

Steve is a positive motivation to all who know him and a living example of what positive attitude can do. He was born in St. Anthony, Idaho in 1948. An Rh negative blood factor resulted in cerebral palsy, which causes motor coordination problems and results in spastic weakness of the extremities.

Steve was raised on a farm outside St. Anthony, which helped him gain physical confidence to do what many with his degree of cerebral palsy wouldn't attempt. A few examples of his many physical interests include riding and training horses, camping and survival trips, and snowmobiling.

Intellectual pursuits have also been successful. After graduating from St. Anthony High School in 1970 he attended Ricks College. There he was very active in the Discovery program, a biological field camp. Strong in his spiritual beliefs, Steve taught religion for this program.

In 1972, Steve went on to Brigham Young University, where he graduated in 1975 in Sociology and Psychology. While at the "Y" Steve became very involved in the survival program and proved that disabled people could successfully participate in that strenuous activity. He then helped bring the survival program idea to Ricks College.

Steve is now pursuing a Masters Degree in Counseling and Guidance at BYU and hopes to work at the junior college level. His great motivation in life comes from a strong belief in the gospel of Jesus Christ.

K.J.K.

Chapter 14

The Pool

By Steven Anderson

"You can climb the highest mountain, one step at a time."
　　　　　　　　　　　　　　—John Wanamaker

The center was clear, blue and dark. With water rising from deep within the earth, the spring had formed a pool. The algae which grew around its edges gave way deeper to a gold-silver sand. Even deeper it changed to the deep, dark, blue which gave the pool character, as did the gentle slope covered sparingly with alpine fur, high mountain grasses, and flowers. The outcropping rock gave it dimension. The water ran from the pool into a stream, tearing and rippling away like a rebellious child in the high country as if its only law was change and brutality edged on by gravity. But up on top was peace, surging upward in the deep blueness of the pool.

It was here I rested. Letting my lungs and muscles gather strength, and my mind take in all that my senses would and more, I soon realized my being was taking on the upward surge of the pool. And soon it was as though the pool and my innermost parts were the same, something I neither feared or understood.

I could understand my fatigue; the hike had been long, steep, and treacherous. The air had thinned. And the sun had hit me hard with its heat. All the way up it had been me and the Fox

Canyon trail at odds. Set into battle, upward I had climbed, cursing each rock I had stumbled over, cursing my imperfect body for not being more cooperative, and cursing myself for getting the crazy idea to climb to Fox Spring in the first place. But now the battle was over. I had not won, yet the Fox had not won either. And now, by the pool, I knew the Fox had not fought me. I had fought myself, and the Fox had just been there, trying me, watching me to see if I would overcome...or defeat myself. And I was for a moment one with the pool, canyon, earth, and perhaps the universe.

Memories came and went with the surging ripples of the pool. I could hear feelings that were never spoken...

"Mrs. Anderson, I don't mean to be hard but with cerebral palsy there is a high rate of mental retardation..."

"No, Steve, will never learn..."

"There may be a chance of helping him but..."

"If I were you I'd place him with his own kind..."

"Just leave him here and go on living your life."

"But I can't. Don't you people understand, I can't."

"Melva, I want to see Steve walk before I die...but mostly I want you and Lee to accept him and quit running all over the country looking for a miracle..."

"Yes, Mother, you're right."

"Look Mom, Dad has Steve on his horse. That darned brat is learning to ride before he can walk..."

"Look, Grandma, Steve's walking!"

The memories were coming more clearly now. And feelings were knife sharp. My friends were the animals of the earth.

"Mom, that youngest son of yours put a snake in my bed."

"Steve, would you teach that dog of yours some manners?"

"Lee, that boy of yours and his horse think alike."

"Steve, I've got to get rid of your hawk."

"But Dad...let him be free..."

"Alright son, I'll be kind if you'll be brave."

"Got a deal, Dad!"

And then the knife struck.

"School! What the devil for? Why?"

"Because we feel it's time."

"Alright, but he'll be home for summer...maybe one day he'll go with you kids."

"Damn right the brat will."

"And don't swear, Judith."

I could see in the pool...hurt, doubt, courage, and determination of a family set on a trail like that of the Fox to make life endurable for its youngest member, and the youngest member getting set for battle against himself. It was known to the family that I was intelligent and capable...but the rest of the world was like Fox trail—cold rock that shouted in my ears: "Show me!"

It took me some time to realize that the shouts were not all from outside my being, the major percentage were from within. The inevitable battle began on the plains of spirituality and intellect. Where would it end?...there would be no end.

I was sent away from home nine months out of the year for five years, and voices and feelings were in the pool...

"Now say a, e, i, o, u...very good!"

"Come on now, can do are the words."

"Good boy, you'll be able to write one day."

"Steve, for pete's sake, catch the stupid ball...even Benny can do that."

"All I can say, Mrs. Anderson, is that your son is certainly not mentally retarded in any way; but he does have a stubborn streak in him..."

"You know what the little devil did yesterday...climbed over the fence and went to town...said he just wanted a look around."

"Can anybody beat him at checkers?"

And when summer came I was with my horse and dog and that was all that mattered. The horse was a bay-mare my father gave me as a birthday present, the dog was a young, grey Heinz 57. And the three of us were either saints or criminals. But during the summer we were inseparable companions, having good times and paying for the trouble, but it wasn't much trouble...

I turned from the pool to the sky—a clear, deep, blue of another shade. Yes, there were events, statements...but there were feelings in all these. Feelings of estrangement, of alienation, and of aloneness. But these were usually taken over by anger, accomplishment, and love. Anger overcame estrangement that people labelled me with, which eventually lead to tolerance. Alienation was overcome by accomplishment and perhaps compensation showing at first others, then myself, that I could do anything I wanted to. And aloneness was overcome by love of life and living life's experiences. There were feelings which would always be hard to explain in words. Laughter and tears were the best defenses for such things.

My lungs were getting used to the high country now. My muscles were going through a rejuvenation process. But as I looked back at the pool, I knew I wasn't ready to leave. There were more images in the rippling liquid...

"Can I play football, Coach?"

"'No!"

"We won't play unless Anderson is on the team."

"Alright."

"Can I play baseball, Coach?"

"Like football, Anderson, yea."

"Virginia, would you like to go to the Prom?"

"With you? You're crazy!"

"Sharon, the Prom's Saturday night, want to go?"

"Sure, Steve, when will you be over?"

"Dad, I just can't."

"Are you sure son? C'mon—You're no quitter."

The pool echoes back and forth across time. Suddenly I became restless. I knew there were other canyons, other pools, and higher country I wanted to see. I took what peace I could and prepared to travel on. As I did so, I knew I was the pool and the stream and the trail, and the higher country was a plateau not yet reached. But the pool stayed there. I was moving on.

The Beginning

*S*ue had a normal life until she reached junior high school age. Then suddenly, and without any apparent reason, she began to have epileptic seizures. Soon her life began to change, as the seizures became more and more frequent. She began to feel frustrated and insecure and was afraid to go places for fear she would have a seizure. Her parents sought medical and psychological help, but the reason for the trouble was not easily found and Sue could not seem to make people understand that she had no control over the situation.

It was a long, difficult battle before the cause of the problem was uncovered, but Sue continued to have faith that some day it would be remedied. She tells of the limitations and disappointments which she must face during her growing up years, how she encountered rejection and misunderstandings from her friends, and finally how she endured the many tests and surgery which were necessary to gain control of her problem. Through it all, Sue has continued to show courage and hope, and we see that along with her sweet spirit and shining personality there has emerged a stronger spiritual outlook in her life. She has found that life can be beautiful even when there are shadows which we must look beyond, and that we must never give up hoping that our dream will some day come true.

S.A.H.

Chapter 15

Look Beyond the Shadows

By Susan Parkin LeBaron

"For they can conquer who believe they can."
—Dryden

Until I experienced epilepsy, the illness was a complete mystery to me. I had heard about it and like everyone else, I thought it was some dreadful disease. People just freeze when they hear about epilepsy. They think if they touch anybody who has it they'll be contaminated, and that's what I thought.

I was quite young when it started. I had never seen a person have a seizure, nor had I ever studied about it in school. I connected it with mental retardation, as I knew that retarded people frequently have convulsions.

I don't really remember my first seizure. I was at school and when I realized that something was wrong, I was rather frightened because I didn't know what had happened. My mother came and took me home, and I thought it was just some kind of temporary illness.

The seizures happened again and again. As they began to get more frequent, people would explain what they were like and I began to really get uptight. People would stare like I was a freak or something, and it was as if ten thousand eyes were on me.

My self-confidence really went down. I was just at that junior high age, when it's hard to find yourself anyway. I was scared to death to go anywhere—to a movie, to the grocery store with Mom—afraid I would have a seizure. It's very hard on you when you come out of one. It absolutely petrified me! Of course, my parents were very worried, as parents would be. They took me to the hospital for medical help. There I was asked many questions and given tests, but the brain wave test was completely normal and so the first diagnosis was not epilepsy. They did not know what was wrong.

I was told by a psychologist that I was probably just doing it to get attention. I couldn't seem to make anyone understand that I couldn't do anything about it. That was one of the hardest things I had to face—the fact that no one would believe that I had no control over it. I became very upset and very frustrated at times because I felt that I was trying so hard and yet I couldn't seem to control it.

I can see now why my parents felt as they did. There was no evidence of a reason for the seizures. If I had a child that way, I would probably just shake my head and say "When is she going to grow up?" But that was before I knew what I know now.

It was terribly difficult for a few years. When I wasn't on medication I had seizures right and left. Some of my friends were told to stay away from me. It made me feel very badly. It was hard to adjust to being an epileptic. I'd see my friends being cheerleaders and I was very envious of them. I often had several seizures in one day, and after two or three days of that I would feel so low that I would think, "Why me? Why does this have to go on?"

When I was in the ninth grade I began to get a little confidence. I was asked to be on the seminary board and also to be vice president on the council. I loved it. It seemed to have a very good effect on me, knowing that I was a part of things. It really gave me a feeling of being somebody, and now I felt that my problem was something I could gradually overcome.

I became as involved as I could. At school I explained to my teachers about my problem and they were all very considerate. When I could walk into a classroom and have confidence in the teacher—if I knew that the teacher would take it "with a grain of salt," then it was no big deal if I had a seizure while I was there.

The students were sometimes more difficult. Some were understanding, but some were the kind who would stick their noses up in the air and treat me like I was dirt.

There's one important thing I learned—we are all different and even when we don't have seizures, some people don't like our personalities. So we ought to allow one quirk, one mistake or problem in anybody's personality.

I found that after a seizure I could accept the looks from my friends. I learned to relax and tell them, in modern terms, "hang it in your ear!" I had looked at many of my friends and thought they didn't have a problem in the world, but I came to realize that I wasn't the only one with problems. Though theirs were not always visible, some of them were worse than mine. As they became older, my friends began to also realize that the world is full of problems—it's an imperfect world out there. We must all learn to live in it. Some day we will have to teach our children to live it in, too. When I have children I hope to be able to explain to them about the things they will experience. If a family sees a person walking with a white cane, the mother should explain that the person cannot see, but that the rest of the person is all right. She should tell the children that none of us are perfect, but that we are all the children of God and he loves us, no matter what our imperfections are.

I have two brothers and one sister. My mom and dad treated us pretty much the same, although Mom was afraid for me. I think Dad helped her a lot. He'd say, "Let her be. Let her do her own thing." One time we were up in Idaho at a place where there was a very large bridge. I decided to jump off it, and I got a big kick out of it. I didn't know that Mom was having a heart attack but Dad just got hold of her and told her to let me go.

Parents need to use common sense, of course, but if they overprotect, that can cause more problems. It is good for parents to help their child to get involved with things. My piano helped me a lot and brought me a great deal of confidence. It is good for anyone to be able to do something they can be proud of and to see something that they have accomplished.

I know now that in a way, my problem has been a blessing in my life. It has made me realize that everyone has trials—some more trying than mine. Sometimes when I hear about other people's troubles I realize how lucky I am. When I got in college I began to really get my thoughts together; I realized who I was and why I was here and I knew that things could be a lot worse.

My problem has opened my eyes and helped me to be more compassionate and understanding of other people. I have a great desire to help others in any way that I can. Many times during my struggles I fell to my knees and drew close to my Father in

Heaven. I prayed earnestly about my situation, and I have been blessed with a strong testimony. My spiritual development has increased tremendously.

President Nathan E. Tanner has said that life wasn't meant to be easy. But there is much that can be accomplished from our weaknesses and trials. It is our duty to make the most of what we have, in the best way we can. If we have the right attitude, the right perspective on life, if we know who we are and we try to fill our potential, we can partly wash away our troubles. We can know that in the next life we will not have them. We can be perfect.

Another important thing I've learned is that we must endure whatever comes to us. Some people have anything they want, and it's hard for them to go to their Father in Heaven in prayer, no matter what their problem is. I know that if you make it a matter of daily prayer that you can endure to the end.

A little over a year ago, after a great deal of testing and studying my case, it was decided that I should have an operation to try and correct my problem. I was terribly frightened and yet it was exciting because I had reached the point that I felt I would do anything to get rid of the seizures. I was admitted to the hospital, where I spent several weeks being tested and studied. They implanted over twenty electrodes two inches into my brain, in an effort to locate the exact problem area. I think this was the greatest physical and emotional trial of my life. I had to lie flat on my back and endure the pain from the electrodes in my head, while machines recorded the functions of my brain. Finally the doctors decided that surgery was the answer.

I had quite long, dark hair which I was rather proud of, and one day the nurse came in and told me that it had to all be cut off. They shaved my head and I shall never forget that feeling when I went into the bathroom and looked into the mirror. The tears welled up in my eyes and rolled down my face. I wondered then whether it was all worth it, but after that initial shock I was able to get hold of myself and adjust to it quite well. There was another girl there who had to have an operation for a brain tumor. She never could adjust to having to have her hair shaved off. She couldn't even bring herself to look into the mirror.

The surgery was performed in December. I can't remember Christmas at all. I guess my parents went through a very hard time, as I developed a blood clot and it was some time before they knew whether or not I would live.

Now that it is over, I see that my hospital experience was a great learning period for me. I gained a great deal of spiritual growth. People seemed to admire my standards and could see that I had a great deal of faith. I have always believed that someday I would overcome my problems. I had received a wonderful patriarchal blessing at one time which has been a great source of strength to me. It stated that I would someday overcome my affliction completely. Whether it will be in this life or the next, I do not know, but it has been something I have always been able to cling to. It has given me courage and hope when I was sometimes very discouraged and ready to give up. I feel that I have already been greatly blessed, even though the surgery did not entirely do away with the seizures, they are almost completely controlled; and I truly feel in my heart that things will continue to improve and that it *will* be in this life that I will be free of them. I know that patience is the key—*Patience* with a capital "P."

There is still a wonderful part of my story to be told. I feel that it is the best part. About two-and-a-half months after my surgery, I had a strong desire to return to Brigham Young University and be with other young people. I decided one night to go to a road rally. I was feeling very alone and discouraged and the branch president told me to go out and mingle with the people. "Maybe you'll meet someone special," he said. He didn't know how right he was. None other than "Prince Charming" came riding by on his white horse and swept me completely off my feet. He came up to me and began to talk, and he was so handsome and charming that I felt I had known him always. I am usually not this way with people that I do not know, but it was so easy to talk to him. He told me later that he, too, felt that he had known me for a long time. We wonder if we might have known each other in the pre-existence. That is how it seemed.

He walked me home and the following Tuesday he asked me out to a movie. From there a beautiful romance developed. We both fell in love right from the first and became engaged two months after we had met. In four months we were married in the Salt Lake Temple and I know now how Cinderella must have felt. Ray is very understanding of my condition—I could never ask for anyone more kind, more considerate or more wonderful. I told him all about myself the first time we went out together. I thought it was only fair. But he fell in love with me anyway, and I realize how very blessed I am. I know that my patriarchal blessing is being fulfilled. I was promised that I would marry and have a family, and I hung on to that through all the dark and discouraging days. I have experienced a great deal in my young life, both good and bad. Sometimes I have wondered why. Many times I have wished it could be otherwise. But now I see how very fortunate I am. I know that my adversities have been my strengths, for through them I have developed character and have gained spirituality. There were many times in my life that were filled with despair, but I never really gave up hoping that someday things would be better. I know that is what brought me through.

I had one characteristic which made me different than most other girls, the one which I could not control, but in all other ways I was just like anyone else. I wanted to meet a wonderful guy someday and have him say to me, "It doesn't matter that you have a problem—I love you for the person you are."

Now I have found him, and if anyone asked me I would truthfully say, "I would go through it all again, if I knew that he would be there waiting." I always knew that somewhere there was someone for me.

Note:

When the parents of a defect child face the reality of that defect in their much-loved offspring, they don't always think alike and agree on every point. This can be very positive, for it shows that two people are thinking. They will not always have the same strengths and where one is weak, the other may be strong. Through the struggles and confusion come positive direction. The child is the benefactor of this situation, for the parents, working together, lay a strong foundation for their child's success.

Such is the story of the Parkin family of Salt Lake City, Utah. The Parkins first met while attending the University of Utah. Life later led them to St. Louis, Missouri where Dr. Parkin successfully completed dental school. When their beautiful little daughter, Susan, began having seizures, the search for the cause commenced immediately. That search, and the emotions, trials, and errors that went with it, show some very typical patterns that parents with similar situations can relate to. Charles and Christine Parkin tell their stories individually to enhance the above points.

The Father's Story

The initial onset of Susan's seizures was received with great concern by all members of the family. She was hospitalized for

tests which gave her parents some inkling as to some of the possibilities. An analysis was made of the diagnostic tests that were
run at the hospital and the one neurosurgeon indicated there was
a possibility of epilepsy. The neurologist indicated that the EEG
was negative and came to the conclusion that epilepsy was not a
factor. After discussion with several other physicians and one
psychiatrist, it was decided that there was no organic evidence
for epilepsy.

This was comforting to us, as Susan's parents, but led to
conclusions that were actually erroneous. The psychological
impact of epilepsy was, for all practical purposes, rejected mentally by the family. I began to seek for ways by which we could
treat that which was referred to as conversion hysteria. It was
recommended by one of the physicians that we engage the
services of a clinical psychologist. He felt that since there was no
organic evidence of electronic emissions that Susan could be
mentally conditioned to abort the onset of seizures. There were a
few times when this did occur. As an example, on one occasion
some six years after the initial seizure, Susan was skiing in a
group instructional program. She had a seizure which
precipitated a phone call to me with the instructor stating that if
her seizures continued, he would not allow her to continue with
the skiing lessons. She had no more seizures while skiing. There
were a few other instances of this kind, and we were assured by
the psychologist that at no time would she involve herself with
seizures which would in any way endanger body, limb, or life.
However, the seizures increased in frequency and intensity which
frustrated both the physician as well as the psychologist.

We began to realize that our daughter did in fact have
epilepsy and that it was a peculiar type called psycho-motor
seizures.

After an extensive neurological examination, the neurologist
felt that the seizures were eminating from the right temporal lobe
and that a right temporal lobectomy should be performed. She
was admitted for surgery at the University Hospital. I did not feel
comfortable with the circumstances and asked for a second
opinion. A conference was held involving two neurologists, one
psychiatrist, and myself. It was the opinion of the consulting
neurologist that the team that was to perform the surgery did not
have sufficient information to justify a right temporal lobectomy.
It was later found out at UCLA Medical Center that Susan's left
temporal lobe was not entirely active, which meant that if the
right temporal lobe had been removed, Susan's memory banks

would not have been functional. This would mean that though Susan would be capable of cerebration, which would allow her problem solving ability, it would be necessary for her to relearn the solution to each problem every time it confronted her; that is, if the right temporal lobe had been removed, it would be necessary for her to learn to tie her shoe each morning as though it were a new experience. When the UCLA team discovered this, it was then decided that a partial lobectomy be performed. The surgical procedure was initiated and the seizures have not been experienced since that time.

The sociological impact on the family varied with each member. The younger children seemed to accept it without great difficulty. Susan's mother, who was present more frequently when the seizures occurred, was more deeply affected and carried a degree of embarrassment when they did occur. I felt this at times, but I felt that I was shielded more than Susan's mother as I had a deeper understanding of the medical implications involved in the case. I was present on many occasions when Susan had seizures. One example of this was on a trip to Mexico where Susan and I had traveled; she experienced at least eight seizures one day with varying intensities. All of these were experienced in public places. I felt no particular embarrassment nor need to withdraw.

Susan probably had the most severe psychological adjustments to make. Outside of the family, she was experiencing various degrees of rejection. Before the seizure pattern became apparent, Susan had been well accepted in the neighborhood by various boys and girls. Little by little, this changed, causing personality defense mechanisms in Susan which worsened the problem. The young and old did not understand the mechanism of seizures and, as a result, each individual who witnessed them seemed to react by wanting to withdraw and be away from the situation, if at all possible. Much of this problem could have been avoided had we just realized that her epilepsy was totally an organic problem. Had she been given proper doses of medication to better control her seizures, many of her psychological problems could have been avoided. Much of the stress on members of the family could also have been avoided.

In summary, from our own experience, I would recommend certain steps be taken, and the avoidance of other courses of action by family groups involved in this problem:

1. In the event that an adult or child is faced with seizures, seek consultation with a competent neurologist.

2. Inasmuch as competency depends upon training, experience and dedication (and since capability may vary), it would be wise to receive consultation from a second neurologist. When making a selection, it is suggested that you seek the advice of individuals who are well acquainted with doctors in this field.

3. I would have the findings of the attending neurologist rechecked periodically to see if further developments have occurred as a result of the maturity of the child or any biological degeneration such as tumors, cysts, or scar tissue which have developed in the brain centers.

4. I would avoid reaching out into heroics by trying treatments from individuals who may have interesting experiences from using untried techniques or healers that may be more interested in your money than in solving the neurological problems.

5. I would seek an understanding of the problem by attending special orientation sessions given by the Epilepsy Foundation or other competent groups or organizations. The more one knows about the problem, the easier it is to understand and bear from a psychological and sociological point of view.

The Mother's Story

Our first baby passed away at two weeks of age in January of 1951. This sadness was followed by a miscarriage one year later. You can imagine my joy when Susan was born on January 24, 1955, a beautiful baby girl with lots of black hair. She had more than her share of infant and childhood infections and I later regretted not recording them, especially when I was always asked about injuries, high fevers, birth trauma, and other information.

On Halloween Day, just before Susan turned nine, her teacher sent her on an errand out to her car and Susan later told me that during this errand she experienced blurriness of vision. Upon returning to the classroom she had one seizure. This was a very frightening experience to her teacher and the rest of the personnel in the school. That same week another girl experienced a seizure in the same room. Very few of them knew what to do. (All teaching personnel should be schooled in how to care for a patient with a seizure. The first thing most people think of is to prevent the patient from swallowing his tongue but I was taught to just lay the patient on his side.) When I arrived at the school they brought her out in a blanket and put her in the back seat of my Volkswagon. Her seizure had stopped. No one even offered to go with me. I came straight home and called my husband, who immediately came home. We dashed to a neighboring medical center and waited for a doctor, but he never showed up. We decided to take her to the LDS Hospital. She had a seizure in the car on the way up and it was only on one side. When the doctor asked us what side it was, we couldn't remember. (Parents should notice details in a child's illness).

When Susan was 13 her seizures began again, and this time they never quit. In the beginning they occurred about every three days. When she received treatment at the University Hospital they occurred about every seven days, and occasionally she was even free of them for as long as ten days. How Susan and I stayed sane and endured through the first four years of this illness I will never know. My husband described in detail the errors that were made at the beginning. If I had had my way I would have taken her to every neurologist in the city and then I would have traveled to major medical centers.

After the doctor at the University Hospital committed himself to working closely with Susan, she went on heavier doses of medication. That summer she was seizure-free for three months. During this time Susan did volunteer work, working with the mentally retarded, which was a most rewarding experience. That fall the seizures returned, but she made pep club and seemed to have lots of fun. I do not agree with my husband when he says her problem could have been solved with heavier doses of medication. She certainly did live a more normal life when the heavier doses were administered, but Susan's seizures were like clock work and they never left for very long. She was considered to be a patient that had uncontrolled seizures.

I helped Susan a great deal. My husband felt that I overprotected her, which may be possible, but I feel that whatever we did we couldn't have been too wrong because Susan came out of it with lots of strengths. I would help her with her typing and often helped her organize her time and work. I gave her very few responsibilities at home as far as housework is concerned. She took piano lessons and ballet lessons. I believe that a handicapped child needs to learn to excel. I would see that she would eat well and saw to it that she had her rest at night. Proper rest is very important for this type of illness.

I did not accept too many responsibilities out of the home because I needed to be home when the school called. I certainly tried to live a normal life and did so. My husband was always gone a great deal with his work and I felt that one of us needed to be home with the children.

The other children loved Susan and the seizures did not get too embarrassing for them until they grew older. By that time the seizures were better controlled.

I tried to keep Susan home during her seizure period but she was persistent and was determined she was not going to stop living. One of the most difficult problems for her, and still is, was not being able to drive a car. However, she managed to take the driver's course.

Susan was a very courageous young lady, and I guess this is why she was able to survive. She did suffer in her self-image during the earlier part of her life but the Lord strengthened her. He makes us a promise that He will not give us more to bear than what we can live with. She was given a blessing the night before her surgery and I can say that she had absolutely no fear before her surgery.

When I learned about Susan's problem I read a great deal about it and also attended classes at the LDS Hospital given by the Epilepsy Foundation. Psycho-motor seizures exhibited the most bizarre-type behavior and were the hardest to treat with medication. One of the young girls I met at UCLA had this same type of seizures. She would stand on a chair and raise her right arm. Once she was on a bridge and threw her purse into the ocean. The encyclopedias also mention that they may pull at their clothing or start to undress. Susan did the latter only once. Very few people understand that this bizarre-type behavior would be part of seizures and it was very difficult for me to live with them. I certainly intend to do volunteer work when my family is raised for the Epilepsy Foundation.

I feel that lay people should be educated in handling seizures and all other kinds of handicaps, and this should begin in school. People are so fearful of seizures. All Susan needed was about five minutes to find out who she was and where she was after a seizure and she was fine. If people who were with Susan during her seizures would have understood this, they could have helped her greatly. My prayer is that people will take time to understand and know how to help the handicapped.

*W*hat is it like for a child who was born deaf to suddenly be able to hear the many sounds of a busy, noisy world? How easily can he accept his new and frightening existence?

Richard did not hear until he was five years old. In many ways, he had to begin learning all over again. He had acquired many bad habits from having a hearing problem and his development was somewhat different than that of a normal child. Richard struggled through the experiences of a deaf child in a hearing world, and with special education and the aid of a hearing device, he has been able to adjust to his special problem. The help of patient teachers has played a great part in his life. He has been able to work steadily toward the goals which he has set for himself, even though at times he became discouraged and felt very much alone. His frank discussion gives the reader an insight into the successes that have built a positive self concept for him.

Through the love of his parents and by becoming active in church responsibilities, Richard has been able to find his place in the world. He may not acutely hear the sweet song of the bird, but he hears the song of the heart. He knows that "my soul delighteth in the song of the heart; yea, the song of the righteous is a prayer unto me, and it shall be answered with a blessing upon their heads." (D & C 25:12)

The reader will sense, in the last few paragraphs, a shrinking of the handicap of a young man who understands the purpose of life.

K.J.K.
S.A.H.

Chapter 16

Coping With Deafness

By Richard Moore

"To climb steep hills requires slow pace at first."
—*Shakespeare*

I was born deaf in the state of Delaware in 1952. The cause of my deafness was anoxia (lack of oxygen). My parents didn't find out until I was about three years old. I was fitted with my hearing aid when I was about five years old. It was the first time that I really entered the world of sound. I was astounded at the noisy world. I had to learn the different sounds and where their source was.

I started going to kindergarten with some hearing children. At first it was a new experience for me, being away from home without my parents. I was successful in overcoming my fears and made lots of friends in that school. As time went by, I entered the special education department in the city of Wilmington. I progressed greatly there and overcame many bad habits and behaviors. I received my speech training there, having to catch up on what I missed during the time without my hearing aid. I struggled and fought to overcome the problems that I had.

I couldn't accept what I was at that time. I thought that I was the only deaf person in the world and was ashamed of myself. I sometimes thought that my parents were to blame. I finally realized it wasn't their fault at all, but I often wondered why I was deaf. As time went by, however, things unfolded before me.

I entered third grade in a public school, which was another new experience for me. It was also the giant step to my success in overcoming fear and problems. The teachers there changed my life, along with my parents who had great patience with me through those tormenting years of schooling. I finally made it through elementary school. I'm sure that my parents had great rejoicing in their hearts. I had passed the first hurdle of my life towards my goals. My years of junior high school seemed like a dueling contest in the classroom, with changing classes, large classrooms, and lack of attention compared to what I had been getting.

All this loaded up to a great amount of frustration which I had to carry. I certainly had my parents worried to death, but they seemed to hang on and had faith that I would make it. They encouraged me, pushed and pulled on me until finally I graduated from junior high school. During those trying times I developed a great interest in art and drawing.

I applied to enter a technical high school where I could get my training in Art and Advertising. I really wanted to be an artist and be successful in it. During high school I became a loner, and didn't want to associate with my friends much. I always stayed home and worked on my drawings. I didn't really know who I was or why I was deaf. Then, in my senior year in high school, I began to make friends again. I was elected vice-president in the Vocational Industrial Club of America in my school's art department. I was also nominated to compete in the state art contest of the V.I.C.A. This built my self-concept a great deal, and gave me courage to venture even further. After I graduated, I worked for two advertising firms. I received more training in this work, and felt I was on the road to success.

During this time I began to realize who I was, and why I was deaf. I was more active in the LDS Church and began to understand my purpose in life. As I became active in my Church, I received more callings to positions; I was ward art director, a home teacher, assigned to work with the missionaries, and then called to be a part-time stake missionary.

As time went on I finally found myself, knowing who I was and I felt so happy. I knew now that I was somebody and was here to serve for a purpose in life.

I had progressed greatly in my talents in art. I was very happy in my job and I knew that I had finally made it. I look back and can see that it was worth it. Many people thought that I would never succeed. I had surprised many people in the success that I had.

The LDS Church had decided to call me to a full-time mission in the California South Mission. There I found the full meaning of my life. First I was called into the hearing program, but later I was called into the deaf program. I had the opportunity to work with my own people and associate with the deaf. There I learned sign language, which had a great affect on my life. I was much happier, helping the people as I served my Father in Heaven. I was called to be a zone leader and experienced tremendous growth. Soon it was time to go home. I wanted somehow to continue my happiness.

I applied to Brigham Young University and was accepted. Here at BYU I have received more leadership positions, such as vice-president in the Deaf Club. I am now the president of the Club, and delight in watching my deaf brothers and sisters reach out and grow.

I am very proud of what I am and of my deafness. It has taught me many things which I would never have learned if I was hearing. I love my parents for their patience and kindness. If it weren't for them to encourage and push me, I wouldn't be where I am today. They have helped me accept and conquer many challenges and helped me to overcome the problems that have come my way. I know that all deaf people can do it too!! I am very happy that God is with me and has helped me so much.

I am now a student at BYU majoring in psychology. I am also engaged to a deaf girl, a wonderful person, and look forward to marrying and raising a family. We will have special challenges together, but those challenges will be faced and solved.

You see, handicapped people are just people with certain problems. We all have the same needs and wants. Your problems are probably different than mine. Father in Heaven will help us all.

*T*hough blind all of his life, Maurice Bowman has been able to overcome the many obstacles which face a person with this kind of disability. As in many other accounts of this kind, Maurice attributes the success of his life to the fact that he had loving parents who taught him not only to do things of value in his life, but also to enjoy and appreciate the many opportunities available to him. From this he has learned that the world need not be a dark and dreary place, even though one cannot see. With the help of those who care, life can be a happy and rewarding experience.

Maurice has not only enjoyed a pleasant and productive childhood, but has also made a success of his school years and is looking forward to a bright future. With this optimistic attitude, he is sure to find it.

K.J.K.

Chapter 17

My Handicap
is a Blessing

By Maurice Bowman

"Overcome fear by doing what you are afraid to do."
—Nathan Eldon Tanner

In this world of ours, crowded with norms and preconceived stereotypes, can be found the evidence that man intuitively has the drive or will for success. Although this often drives him to his limits, man is sometimes impeded and halted by the limitations of other men's ideas. Such is the fate of many handicapped individuals—to fight against or give way to the concept that when one is handicapped, one can do nothing. How can this battle be won? How can a handicapped individual contribute to the riches of men's souls in society?

The answer begins in the home, for that is where the foundation for an active, dynamic self-concept is laid. Parents of all children, handicapped or not, have the keys for a successful individual and world.

Let me tell you of the challenge which faced my parents—that of raising a blind son. No doubt they had questions and fears. They conquered each of them through careful planning together.

As I recall, my growing up was supported with the tender love and divine council which was reflected in each teaching moment. Their philosophy was the key. I was to be taught the ways of a normal life. My responsibilities should be small at first, growing increasingly more difficult as I grew. I should become independent so as to become able to think, act and live as a normal person, contributing to the world's human family quality.

As I grew older, my father gave me lessons on how to work. Many were the truckloads of dirt or gravel or trash we hauled together. The beauty of the family garden and yard was maintained by my father, with my following his coaching to discover the thrill of accomplishment. I learned the joy of working and seeing the job done and sensing my father satisfied.

Another important part of my growth was through the scouting program. Each new experience with the other scouts added to my character. There is nothing greater than planning the design of a pinewood derby racing car, carving out the shape, sanding the body, painting it, and finally watching it win a prize at the troop level. Nor is there a word to describe the feeling one has of working on cub scout requirements and activities with one's dad and then receiving the award for which he has worked. As I worked on my own and with my parents to earn my scouting ranks, I overcame one of the greatest mountains of my life. It gave me confidence to tackle other challenges.

There was one requirement for the First Class scouting award which was to swim fifty yards. When you fear not only the water but the "unseeable" depths, it's more than a challenge. It was a matter of several years and a patient scout master before I was able to make it happen. I jumped into that unknown and unseen blackness! With my scout master urging me on from the edge, I swam and swam until I made it. I really passed that requirement! But more than just receiving the badge, I gained self-confidence and a knowledge that I could and would do anything that I reasoned to be worth obtaining.

From that experience, I went on to earn my Eagle rank, earning both the swimming and lifesaving merit badges. With the aid of a great merit badge counselor, I also earned the photography merit badge, all of which added more confidence and understanding in and of myself and the world around me.

On my parents' suggestion, I went to the Arizona State School for the Deaf and Blind in Tucson, Arizona. There I learned much from great teachers. Music became my love. I learned to play the cello and string bass and participated in the orchestra and stage band. I was also given the opportunity to serve on the student council.

There was a project at the school to teach the totally blind about the orientation problems on the campus. I was assigned to a great girl who could not find her way across the street from her dormitory to the dining hall. She had little confidence in herself but relied on others for mobility, and many other personal needs. It took her about a semester to learn the campus adjacent to her dorm. I felt sorry for her, because such dependence on others for life's necessities could doom an individual to social death and low self-esteem as well as worthlessness.

After graduating from high school with honors, I went to the University of Arizona and I am currently a senior at Brigham Young University. My major is Distributive Education, and I feel confident I will succeed in my profession.

My successes can be attributed to several factors. One is that my parents treated me as equal to my peers and the other children in my family. My parents taught me the elements of having a good self-concept, one that is directed toward success. Their love showed me I was of worth. They taught me the meaning and worth of work, of doing a job to the best of my ability. This is the thing which gives the handicapped child a sense of responsibility. By teaching him how to work, parents tell their child that he is able to be independent and can be a contributor to the family, the community and the nation.

Whatever you do, don't let your handicapped child feel he can do nothing. Teach him to participate in groups and in society outside the home. Teach him how to work and give him all kinds of experiences with life, making adjustments when necessary. Show him that he can succeed, thus forming a good self-image foundation. There is nothing more important than to have a great self-concept and to learn to succeed in whatever one wants to do in life. In this way, a handicap—even one like blindness—can become a blessing. It can teach us how to succeed and contribute to the lives of others, as they contribute to ours. This is what it has done for me.

$\mathcal{B}$onnie Consolo is an active wife and mother who cooks, sews, writes, drives a car and takes care of her children. Since they were babies, she has fed them, cuddled them and pinned diapers on them as any other mother would do, but Bonnie does it with her feet.

She was born without arms. One foot was also crippled, until her mother straightened it by her tender and constant care. Bonnie was taught by her parents to do everything that other children did, so that she might learn to be independent. She graduated from high school and later attended vocational school, learning bookkeeping and other office skills. She was at one time fitted with artificial arms, but found that they were of no use to her. She decided to just do the best she could with what she had, and that is what she has done.

Through her strong determination and efforts, Bonnie has made her life a success. A man named Frank Consolo saw an article about her in a California newspaper, and he wrote to her. He encouraged her to seek better employment in the state where he lived, and she drove all the way across the country by herself, found an apartment and a job. Soon after that she married Frank, and after many adjustments and some struggles, she has found happiness in marriage and motherhood.

Bonnie and Frank are helping other handicapped people through their special efforts, which includes a film they have made entitled "A Day in the Life of Bonnie Consolo." It has won many awards for its excellence. After learning of her great accomplishments and seeing how she has overcome her difficulties, we could learn a valuable lesson from this very courageous lady.

S.A.H.

Chapter 18

Problems Are Stepping Stones Toward Growth

By Bonnie Consolo

"You can make yourself whatever you will, if you work."
—Anonymous

On October 12, 1938, I was born in the hills of Kentucky. My mother was twenty-four years old, my father twenty-eight. They already had two children, my sister June and my brother Milburn. There were two more born after me. Four of my parents' children were normal. I was not. My right leg made a U-turn and my foot lay up against the outside of my leg. Also, I was armless. Many ventured guesses as to why, but no one really knows.

We were a poor family as far as money goes, but rich in what really counts—love for each other, including me. I was just another of the family. No one felt sorry for me and I was not allowed to feel sorry for myself. Help was given to me when asked for, but otherwise I was left to do things my own way. When discipline was handed out, I got my share.

Instinct told my mother how to handle my problem. Although she had no medical experience, it was she who straightened my leg. Every day, as she cared for me, she gently pushed on my foot until it was straight. From the time I was a baby, my feet took over doing things normally done by hands. Almost everything others do, I can do, thanks to her. She always made me try. She and the rest of my family taught me to be independent and not to think of myself as handicapped.

Of course, there were problems I encountered in growing up. Though I went to the public school and took all the regular curriculum, there were many games I could not join in. When I could participate, however, I was always included. The high school I attended was run by the Presbyterian Church. All the girls were required to wear skirts. I did too, for awhile, because I wanted to be like everyone else. But because I used my feet for so many things, this posed a problem. So, much as I hated it, I was allowed to wear slacks.

The thing that bothered me most was people. They first stared at me in disbelief and then looked at me with "the poor little thing" written all over their faces. This look still appears on the faces of many, but it doesn't bother me anymore. Some mothers of boys I went out with said, either to me or someone else, that they wouldn't want their son to marry an armless girl.

Sometimes I had periods of depression over being different from others. But I learned to adjust my mental attitude as I adjusted physically. Handicaps are mostly in the mind. People sometimes put limits on themselves, but I have not set any limits. I try to learn something new each day, usually some new way of doing something. If someone fights all your battles for you, it takes all the fight out of you.

Some people assume that because I haven't any arms, I must also be unintelligent. On one occasion my girlfriend, Karen, and I went to the department store. Karen had severe muscle problems and was very lucky to be alive. People would ask her what happened to me, and she would tell them, "Ask Bonnie, she can talk." They automatically thought that because I was in the physical condition I was that I must have a mental problem as well.

I tried in every instance I could to prove that this was wrong. When I was a teenager I took the driver's test to obtain a license. When it was over, I asked the examining officer if I would be able to get a license and he said, "You passed the test—I have no choice." I have been driving a car for over 20 years.

Employment has also been a problem on occasion. When I lived in Florida no one would give me a job, except at one place. For two years I worked there, although from the day I walked in, I wanted to walk out. Continually I searched for work outside. The switchboard, which I handled, was constantly ablaze with lights from incoming calls as well as the twenty-five or more offices within.

I had the ability, but no one could see beyond the way I looked. At the end of two years of degradation in that place, a businessman offered me a job as his secretary. It would be less money than I was making, but because I wanted out so badly, I accepted. One week later he gave me a raise, and I knew I had made the right choice. I will be eternally grateful to him for giving me that chance. He started me on the right track towards having confidence in myself.

Later I moved to California, and found just the opposite attitude in hiring practices. There they wanted me for my intelligence and ability, which is all I ever asked for. I took the entrance exam at Pacific Telephone Company with ten other girls. I was the only one accepted. Believe it or not, I even passed the physical exam they required.

On September 22, 1966, I married Frank Consolo. Two months later I found out that I was to realize the answer to my prayers. My most cherished desire was mine. I was pregnant.

For that nine months, I was inwardly floating on a cloud, living with a feeling of ecstasy and grandeur that I had never before known. Even the problems Frank and I had in adjusting to each other could not darken my spirits. Frank's life had been one filled with problems, too, although none of them were physical. When he was a child there was a lack of love and affection. Unless you receive love, it is difficult to give it. Frank tended to be cold and withdrawn while I was warm and loving. I wondered about this. His was a very domineering personality, and I was always on my guard lest he dominate me. His thoughts were very negative while mine were extremely positive. I kept from him the terrible secret the doctor had announced to me. "Did you know there is a big chance that your baby will be born like you?" I was hurled from my feeling of joy into one of great concern. "Your life hasn't been that bad," he said. "You, more than anyone else, would be able to handle it."

"Thank you, but no thank you," I said. There was an excellent gynecologist in town whom I had heard about from a friend. But even he had a difficult time calming my hysteria. My tremendous faith in God was breaking apart. "My Lord," I cried, "why are all these things happening to me?"

Dr. Francis Rene Van de Carr listened patiently as I poured out my problems with Frank and my concerns for my unborn child. He could give me no guarantees as to my baby's condition. His calm mannerism, however, did allow me to return to my original belief that God will make things right. Through all this, I was still happy that I was carrying a tiny life around inside me.

My mother came to spend the last few weeks with me. She said that if I was feeling the baby kick everywhere at once, there was nothing for me to fear. She told me that when she carried me, I kicked only in one place. She was right! When my baby was born, he was the envy of all who saw him. He was perfect in every way. My prayers for my baby had been answered. Frank and I now have two perfectly normal, healthy boys. Caring for my home and family are my greatest joys.

Through all this I learned a great lesson. Problems are steps toward growth. I had come through a tragic time in my life and I am a better person for handling it the way I did. There was a way out, yes. A way too horrible for me to comprehend. A term so ugly I don't like to write it. But there have been women, who, because of their fears, have taken that method. I, perhaps more than most, had reason to fear, but if I had aborted my child, I would have destroyed a beautiful, normal, healthy boy. How *can* anyone?

The feeling of inferiority I had carried with me all my life was slowly dissipating. My faith in God, which began at my mother's knee, was now stronger than ever, and I knew that the only way to find happiness was to continue doing the best I could at everything I could. There can be no such thing as giving up.

My greatest goal in life is to be able to help others. There aren't many things I can do for people, but I hope to be able to give them a better understanding of themselves. I want to encourage them to become self-reliant and to realize that every challenge put in front of us builds character and makes us a better person in handling it.

My problems are not over. When they are, it will be time for me to meet my Creator. But until that time I shall live a full life. I shall go where I want to go and do the things I want to do. People still stare at me, and I realize they always will, but my life will not be wasted worrying about it. All I have ever asked is to be accepted just as another human being, to love and be loved for what I am.

Section Three

Raising a Handicapped Child

Back of the work, back of the sorrow, back of the life, ever grows the ideal. How constantly we keep our eyes upon it determines whether we shall fall as failures along life's highway or fulfill the divine purpose of our being.
—David O. McKay

Chapter 19

Emotional Reaction and Adjustment of Parents of Handicapped Children

The birth of a child is usually an occasion for stress in a family. Mom is experiencing severe discomfort. Dad and the kids struggle with family adjustments, including extra chores and new time schedules. After the delivery, there is a reduction in stress and the family finally gets back to normal.

When a visibly handicapped child is born to a family, however, the stress is usually not relieved by the birth. A handicapped newborn marks a transition to a period of heightened anxiety and sustained indecision. This lowers the threshold to fatigue and tends to upset the family routine.

One reason for the above experience is unrealized expectations. We all think, expecially with our first baby, that it will be a superbaby. While the baby is yet in the uterus, parents are dreaming of Miss USA or a second Jim Thorpe, or a future President of the USA! Everyone silently hopes for a superbaby, but the perfect baby with no blemish whatsoever is a notable exception. Many babies that become highly successful as adults do so out of their need to compensate for personal deficiencies and defects. The parents of these "super-adults" probably wondered if their child would ever make it!

And so many parents, possibly including yourself, are faced with the reality that this new little human being may not measure

162

up to be the "child of your dreams." The parents of children not physically or mentally handicapped usually face it later. You will have to face it sooner.

It seems the key to facing this reality is attitude. A reality is that everyone is born with a potential. Your parents allowed you to reach for your potential, and hopefully your attitudes will allow your limited child to reach for his. A potential coaxed along by nourishment and love will blossom into the person he or she is meant to be. So, let the child of your early expectations fade and let the real child blossom and grow!

Some defects show up at birth, while others show up during the early developmental stages of the child. Some handicaps are not really clear until school age. When the reality finally hits, there is an initial emotional reaction of shock, with several typical adjustment stages to follow. Most parents of handicapped children experience tough moments and struggles. Though we all have a unique situation and different personalities, we all experience the same types of stages.

The inital reaction upon learning of the handicap is one of pure emotion. Normal children many times don't live up to the often unrealistic expectations of their parents, but this is gradual and can be accepted gradually. The diagnosis of a handicap such as mental retardation brings an abrupt end to those expectations. This abrupt end usually causes overwhelming shock. You may experience times of irrational behavior characterized by feelings of helplessness and crying. This is normal and to be expected.

The physician has explained your baby's condition to you and showed you the signs and symptoms. You may refuse to believe it. This is called denial, and is very natural because it helps to cushion the tremendous blow. You do it because you wish to be free of the situation or deny its impact. It is tough to accept the fact that the blueprint of your baby contains some imperfections. You need some time to adjust your expectations of this baby to an acceptable realism. If you have already experienced this stage, don't feel badly about it. Denial is a common defense reaction which is brought on by a stressful situation—it is automatic and unconscious. Remember, it is alright to take some time to accept the situation, but it is a bad thing if your mind never accepts it.

Sometimes you may feel that you can hardly drag yourself around. It's a true case of the blahs, kind of like having the flu. You may experience knots in the stomach and other nagging pains. Food doesn't even seem interesting. You talk to yourself more than usual. Your body is saying, "It's too much!" You need some time out, so escape for a few hours. After you have felt pain for awhile, you may irrationally try to displace this pain by blaming and hurting others. Many parents direct this anger toward themselves or the baby, or outwardly toward hospital staff and other people. It is also common in this stage to experience anxiety and fear for your baby's life. Some parents who experience this feel reluctant to become attached to or interact with their babies. This, of course, is not a healthy situation for the parents or the baby.

Though the above feelings are normal, be careful about acting on this anger. Some people may understand your plight, but many will not. Clashes with acquaintances may cause more guilt feelings and the vicious cycle starts all over again. Especially be careful *not* to start blaming your spouse for this unexpected problem. If you do, there is no way you can work as a team. Teamwork is essential to supply a successful and happy lifestyle for the handicapped child and his family. Don't blame your doctor for "not discovering it soon enough," or for doing a "poor job" of telling you. The news of your child's handicap is going to be painful no matter how you become informed. If you have a doctor who is humanly honest with you, learn to trust and listen to him.

Parental reactions to the diagnosis of a handicap are highly individualistic and vary in intensity of responses and manifestations. These responses depend upon personality, nature of the marriage, parental aspirations for the child, feelings about social class, etc. Two very common experiences of most parents of handicapped children, however, are the "guilts" and the "greats."

Guilt seems to be the most common experience. You may have caught yourself wondering, "What have I done to deserve this?" Most of us see our children as extensions of ourselves. If we have a religious background we may be tempted to regard this handicap as punishment for some sin we have committed. Some parents search back into their lives for that horrible sin that has caused this terrible situation, and they most likely never find it! Some parents even begin to suspect their spouse has sinned and this handicap is a direct act of God because of that sin. The idea is *not* supported by today's religious beliefs.

In most cases the real cause of the handicap largely remains a mystery that must be accepted. Guilt is only reality-based if the parent has truly caused the handicap through an act such as an unsuccessful crude abortion or drug overdose. Guilt is a normal response when we deal with unanswerable questions and is a type of self-punishment.

It is important to move beyond your guilt feelings very early and accept the handicap for what it is. Guilt feelings usually cause us to become very defensive because our personalities attempt to protect themselves. Helpers in the handicapped field may find it hard to break through your defenses to give you the type of help you desperately need.

Sometimes you may have feelings of grandeur about being a "chosen one" to be entrusted to have this handicapped baby. Experiencing the "greats" can be good for parents for awhile. If it develops into a haughty aloofness, however, it can be very damaging to the parent and the child. Yes, you do have a very special mission to perform in helping this handicapped child reach his full potential. This, however, neither puts you above or below parents who don't have a handicapped child.

No one has been able to perfectly describe the pain and anguish felt by parents of handicapped children. It hurts, sometimes more than others. Almost everyone has suffered physical pain that has caused a sleepless night. Pain causes us to be nervous and pace the floor, to toss and turn in bed, to be easily agitated, to even break down and cry. We seek for ways to alleviate the pain. The pain of having a handicapped child may be similar to having physical pain.

When you reach an overwhelming painful state, the body automatically slows down and dulls the senses. As you struggle to adjust, you will find new strength and endurance being developed. Now you find yourself accepting the situation, and love and creativity begin to mold your child's potential.

Some families are not able to successfully work through the hurting pain, and they experience bitterness. This bitterness may spring up in a family when the parents see the child as an obstacle interfering with personal, family, and social desires. Some feel that society is looking upon them as a "defective" family. Some parents even feel bitter about themselves for bringing the child into the world. They may even use members of their community, such as doctors and educators, as scapegoats for this bitterness. This situation is dangerous to the whole family if left unchanged. Acceptance and love are the powers that develop and nuture the handicapped. They cannot be present if bitterness abounds.

Many parents of handicapped children experience ambivalence. Ambivalence means having both positive and negative feelings, or mixed emotions. You may vacillate in your feelings, feeling love and hate for your child at the same time. The reasons for this are many and varied. This usually causes further guilt feelings. You are prone to vacillate in your actions and responses to the handicapped child. Two common actions here are over-indulgence or rejection of the child. Another is putting too much pressure on the child to achieve beyond his level of ability.

Many handicapped children respond poorly to mothering because of disorganized behavior and low frustration tolerance. This also causes ambivalent feelings which may be displaced on other family members, including Dad. The family situation is not conducive to total acceptance of the handicapped child. It seems that the amount of guilt felt by the parents determines the degree of acceptance of the child. Resolve this and live more comfortably!

Another common experience is the feeling of envy of parents who have normal achieving children. This is a natural occurrence and is even felt by the parents of children who aren't handicapped. It is normal to feel envious of other families who seemingly are enjoying a normal life. Envy may be accentuated in community and church social activities. All parents love to discuss the accomplishments of their child. As you fully accept your child's handicap, his smaller and slower accomplishments will give you joy and satisfaction. Your feelings of envy will continually decrease.

Some of us feel repulsed by our handicapped child and reject him in many ways. We feel this repulsion for many reasons. We aren't taught to learn to live with failure, and producing a handicapped child may be regarded by some as a failure. Some may emotionally see a handicap as a result of a committed sin or evil. We all have strong needs for stimulating relationships, and a handicapped child may not be able to give as much in return. It is natural to confine our relationships to those who think, function, and live like ourselves. The list goes on!

The repulsion may end up in various forms of rejection of the child by the parent. Rejection find its origin in the parents' personalities, in the reasons for having the child, and their hopes and plans for the child before he is born. The most common parent personality associated with rejection is perfectionism. If the goals you set for your child are too high for his potential, you are programming him for failure. Your child can't succeed in your eyes or his, and he perceives this as rejection. He then reacts with negative behavior, which you can't tolerate, and a failure cycle evolves.

Another big factor in the parents' acceptance or rejection of a handicapped child is the reason the baby is brought into the world. If the main purpose is to bring life into the world, acceptance comes much easier. If the purpose is to soothe a troubled marriage, the child may end up as the scapegoat and rejected.

Parents show hostility and rejection in many ways. Neglect, blame, ignoring the child's presence, denial of privileges and advantages, humiliation by criticism and ridicule, are some of the ways.

The first important step is to recognize repulsion and rejection, and decide why it is occurring. Next, remember that adjustment is a continual process. Don't be shy about seeking professional help. If you need help—get it!

When problems concerning a handicapped child loom out of proportion, parents may wish they could escape permanently and give up. We are usually ashamed of these feelings and try to keep them hidden, but they do occur to most of us. One painful truance may become blown up out of proportion and engulf the sweetness of life. The natural tendency is to seek to escape, but don't! Time is a great healer.

As parents work through the stages discussed, they come to accept the child and his or her malformation. The baby's normality and strengths take on added significance. This climaxes to the final stage, that of reorganization. This is a very complex and rewarding time during which you find yourself interacting deeply with your child and his or her problems. You will begin to identify similarities between your other children and your baby, which causes increasing attachment. This is an exciting time when the whole family experiences positive growth.

We have been discussing the various stages that the parents of handicapped children may go through. It is true that the birth of a handicapped baby will probably cause some major changes in your way of life. You may have to give up certain things and take on new responsibilities. You will probably find that old ways pass and you mature in new ways. The adventure is in making those new ways positive growth for the whole family.

There will be definite growing pains. Families of handicapped children generally have more problems in individual and marital adjustment, sibling relationships and child-rearing practices. Social, economic and emotional effects are also felt.

But there is the other side of the coin to look at. Having a handicapped child often causes parents to help each other rebuild new, strong spiritual and ethical values. Life priorities and ways of looking at the life experience are deeply affected. Families may experience a "pulling together" and a real closeness.

A handicapped child does not *need* to produce intense family maladjustment. The key is attitude. Attitudes and anxieties have been referred to as social "microbes" and can be very contagious. Your attitudes and anxieties are greatly affected by ignorance about the handicap. The most traumatic period for parents seems to be the period between the time they learn the child is handicapped and the time when they learn what they can do about it. The ideal is to shorten that time span as much as possible.

The way to accomplish this is given by Dr. Thomas Gordon, author of *Parent Effectiveness Training*:

> To accept another "as he is" is truly an act of love; to feel accepted is to feel loved. And in psychology, we have only begun to realize the tremendous power of feeling loved. It can promote the growth of mind and body, and is probably the most effective therapeutic force we know for repairing both psychological and physical damage. [1]

You can make a rich experience out of a tough situation by using bounteous love and acceptance, which will foster maximum growth for the *whole* family.

---

[1] Gordon, Thomas, *Parent Effectiveness Training*, (New York: P.H. Wyden, 1970).

Chapter 20

Parenting of a Handicapped Child

The great majority of babies are born in this country each year without defects. There are, however, more than 200,000 babies born each year crippled, blind, deaf, mentally retarded, diabetic, anemic, or defective in many ways. Specifically, one baby in every 14 born experiences a defect.

It is estimated that there are 15 million Americans whose daily lives are affected by birth defects. Some can be prevented or corrected by present-day medical knowledge. Others who experience defects can lead rich, full lives if their growing-up environment is right. With this in mind, we will explore the prevention of birth defects and the parenting of children born with defects.

Preventing Birth Defects

It is important to understand what we are trying to prevent. The word "handicap" is used interchangeably with "disability" and "defect." Though they do indicate differences in degree, they also imply differences in kind.

A defect is some impairment, imperfection, or disorder of the body, intellect or personality. It may be very serious or be a trivial problem with no adverse effect upon the individual. A disability defect does cause some malfunctioning but does not necessarily affect the individual's normal life. A handicap is a disability which for a substantial period or permanently retards or adversely affects normal growth, development, or adjustment to life.

Having one ear smaller than the other would be a defect, one leg shorter than the other a disability. Handicaps occur when the presence of any defect or disability becomes a source of major concern to the individual. People can be born with defects and disabilities, or acquire them later in life. How they are raised and their consequent attitude is a key factor whether or not the disability becomes a handicap.

There are many different types of defects. Structural defects affect the body's physical shape or size (eg. cleft palate, open spine, club foot). Functional defects involve one or more body parts not working right (eg. cystic fibrosis, muscular dystrophy, color blindness). Inborn errors of metabolism, where the body is unable to convert certain chemicals into others, cause Tay-Sachs disease, P.K.U., and galactosemia. Blood diseases, due to a reduced or missing component or the inability of a component to do its full share of work, causes sickle cell anemia, hemophilia and agammaglobulinemia. The list goes on and on!

What causes birth defects? Many times the answer is unclear or unknown. The major causes are heredity (20 percent) and environmental influences (20 percent). The rest may result from heredity and environment acting together.

Heredity concerns the genetic "blueprints" that a mother and father pass on to their child. Each parent contributes 23 gene-carrying chromosomes to the child's hereditary make-up. The child's uniqueness comes from the specific way in which his father's genes combine with his mother's genes. Not all genes have an equal effect. Some genes "dominate" over others called recessive. The dominant characteristic shows up. These and other factors govern the mechanics of inheritance.

Sex-linked recessive traits, such as color blindness and hemophilia, usually show up only in males. Racial or ethnic traits show up as sickle cell anemia in blacks and Tay-Sachs disease in eastern European Jews. Other examples of inheritable birth defects include diabetes, Huntington's disease and cystic fibrosis.

The environment is that which surrounds the child, even before birth. The nine months between conception and birth is the most important period in our development. During the first 45 days after the ova is fertilized, major body parts and systems take shape. It's a very complicated and fast-paced period of development. Slight errors in building this complicated organ system can be expected here and there. The hope is that these errors won't significantly affect a major structure.

The surroundings of the developing embryo, the fetus, is crucial. Interference from outside, such as poor nutrition or the mother's use of drugs, can affect the development of the baby. Many mothers do not even know they are pregnant during the first six weeks of development. During this time period, the embryo is especially sensitive to environmental influences. Therefore, good day-to-day health habits should be fostered among women who plan to be mothers.

There are three major divisions of environmental influences. The first is direct maternal factors. The mother's general physical and mental health can affect fetal health. Metabolic disorders, such as diabetes, cause mothers to experience more miscarriages, stillbirths, and children with defects. Maternal age is also a factor. Stillbirths are more frequent among young teen-age mothers. Miscarriages and Downs Syndrome (Mongoloid) babies occur most commonly among women 35 years and older. The number and spacing of previous pregnancies may affect the health of the fetus, such as when the mother has several children in close succession.

The second influence is that of environmental causes acting on the mother during pregnancy. Examples include viral diseases and infections, such as German measles (rubella). If this attack takes place during the first trimester of pregnancy, the virus can cause deafness, heart defects, glaucoma, cataracts and central nervous system damage in babies. Venereal diseases can cause blindness (from gonorrhea), bone malformations and organ infections (from syphilis). Almost any type of drug can potentially affect the development of the fetus. A terrible example of this occurred mainly in Europe in the 1960's when thalidomide caused numerous limb deformities in newborns. Today we have evidence accumulating against such commonly used drugs as aspirin, alcohol, and nicotine in tobacco. A mother addicted to heroin or other narcotics will afflict that addiction on her baby. Researchers are yet examining the many effects of drug use upon the growing fetus. Smoking mothers experience more stillbirths, low birthweight babies, and more early infant mortality. Maintaining a balanced diet is essential in the development of a healthy baby. Either a lack of, or improper balance of, food produces more stillbirths, premature and underweight babies, and even inadequate brain development, resulting in mental retardation.

The third influence is the larger environment that surrounds the mother. Pollutants, for example, may affect the organs of the fetus. In Minamata, Japan, a large industry poisoned offshore waters with methyl mercury. Crippling neurological defects were more frequently found among the babies of women who had eaten contaminated fish from these waters. Different types of radiation, such as X-rays, have been linked with deformities to varying degrees.

Now that we have some idea of what causes birth defects, let's examine ways to prevent some of them. The preventive steps are presented in the following format for quick comprehension.

1. Seek professional prenatal care as soon as you suspect you are pregnant. Remember that the baby's life begins at conception.
2. Take steps to prevent the occurrence of contagious diseases such as rubella.
3. Have regular, thorough examinations, including blood tests to check the Rh factor and blood pressure.
4. Be very careful about drug usage and subjecting yourself to X-rays. Talk to your doctor and dentist carefully about this.
5. Overcome any chronic diseases or make sure they are controlled before becoming pregnant.
6. Talk to your obstetrician about his avoiding strong anesthetics during birth.
7. Good care during the birth of your baby may prevent anoxia (lack of oxygen).
8. Have an excellent pediatrician examine your baby. Early diagnosis of any problems during the first hours after birth (eg. Rh incompatability) is essential and may prevent complications from occurring.
9. Know if you have any lead-containing paint in your home. If you do, don't let the baby chew pieces of this paint.
10. Make sure all infections, such as encephalitis and meningitis, are treated early with antibiotics. Recognize early signs of infections and seek competent medical aid.
11. Become safety-conscious for the prevention of head injuries. If your child experiences recurrent headaches, swelling that stays, or sight and hearing complaints, seek good medical attention.

12. If you suspect any heredity diseases or problems which seem to run in the family line or your race or ethnic group, seek genetic counseling.

13. The support of medical research and encouragement of the local use of research knowledge is imperative.

14. Make sure the following are accomplished after your child is born:

    a. Be sure a PKU test and follow-up test is given.

    b. Follow a good immunization program.

    c. Have regular medical examinations of your child.

    d. Be familiar with the early warning signs of possible defects such as the inability of the baby to hold up its head, or to sit up, crawl, walk and talk at the appropriate ages, or the inability to respond to sound or to grasp things.

A New Problem Arises

We assume a newborn will be normal. The great majority of babies are. Once a birth defect or potential handicap is identified however, the parents must deal with several major issues, such as:

1. How to face their own anger, depression and sense of guilt successfully, so they can be as competent and loving parents as possible.

2. How to assure that the handicapped child gets the best possible social and medical care available without driving the child too hard.

3. How to bring the rest of the family into the loving and caring of this child so that his brothers and sisters who are normal will neither resent him nor feel neglected themselves.

The emotional reactions and adjustments of parents of a handicapped child has already been discussed in a previous chapter. Our purpose in this section is to discuss the detection, treatment and day-to-day parenting of the handicapped child.

Detection and Treatment

Many birth defects are visually apparent at birth, such as cleft palate, club foot, or mongolism. Others are less obvious at birth because they affect internal body structure or chemistry.

If there is any suspicion that the fetus in utero has a defect, a process called amniocentesis can be performed to collect fetal cells for examination. This procedure involves taking a sample of the amniotic fluid which surrounds the fetus, using a hypodermic needle passed through the mother's abdominal wall and into the uterus.

Other defects don't show up until later in life, such as Huntington's chorea and diabetes. The first sign is when the symptoms appear. At this point doctors may be able to alleviate some of the symptoms or keep the condition from getting worse. Detection of the defect is the first step, the next being how to treat the defect so as to minimize its effects.

Only a few disorders can be cured, such as structural malformations (cleft palate). There is simply no way to eliminate the basic abnormality of most defects. The great majority of defects, however, can be treated to reduce harmful effects to keep them from becoming worse. The children can then lead fairly normal lives.

There are three major types of treatment (therapy) now in common use. Chemical regulation is used to offset metabolic (body process) imbalances caused by metabolic errors the child is born with. This therapy may include drug treatment such as insulin therapy for diabetics, or special diets for victims of PKU and galactosemia.

Corrective surgery is effective in overcoming structural defects such as cleft lip, club foot and certain heart malformations. Organ transplants and tissue grafts are also used successfully.

The third type of therapy is rehabilitative training. Many defects can be aided by mechanical or cosmetic prostheses, such as braces, artificial limbs, hearing aids and glass eyes. An exciting new development of biochemical engineering is centering research and development in still highly theoretical areas of cellular, genetic and molecular engineering. When perfected, these possible techniques will allow medical science to treat inborn errors of metabolism and blood diseases by replacing or repairing defective genes, enzymes and cells. The future is extremely bright concerning the detection and treatment of birth defects.

The Day-to-Day Parenting

The key to successful therapy for a defect is early detection of the problem. Potentially the parents are the best "detectors" of a handicap. The legendary "maternal instinct" should have more attention paid to it by laymen and medical professionals alike. Often it is the mother who has the first suspicion that all is not well with her child. If a defect is suspected, have the far-sighted courage to tackle its investigation. Trying to ignore the problem will only produce sleepless nights of anxiety. Go to medical professionals for diagnosis. Well-meaning relatives and neighbors who suggest "don't worry about it" or he will "grow out of it" are really doing a disservice, if for no other reason than that this is unlikely to allay the parents' anxiety, which itself may have an adverse effect on the child's emotional development.

A contrasting situation involves parents who suspect a child's disability but pretend, even to themselves, that all is well. They may deliberately attempt to conceal the true situation from the child's pediatrician. This isn't facing reality! The sooner the parents seek help, the better off both they and their child will be.

There are some very typical parental reactions toward a recently-confirmed defect in their child. Some say, or think, "it's too much too soon. I have my life to live." Some parents feel they are too nervous and will never have the patience to work with their handicapped child. Others deny reality or have unrealistic optimism, such as "Billy is doing extremely well" when in fact he isn't. Some feel the weight so heavy they give up as a lost cause and state "it's hopeless, we expect nothing." Many parents quickly project the blame on someone else, such as each other or on their doctor! Some show feelings of guilt by saying "I blame myself completely." These guilt feelings frequently cause parents to adopt a martyr or "chosen couple" complex which is not healthy. They may then go on looking down upon others, and the parents isolate themselves. Usually other people are more accepting than parents realize. Their isolation can become the cause for the child and his family eventually not being accepted. Parents should be willing to discuss the child's problem when the occasion arises and realize that the suspected feelings of others are often a reflection of their own.

Many things can happen to a couple with a handicapped child that gives them the opportunity to blame others. The question is not "who is to blame," but how can we accept this crisis and help our child.

Sometime soon after the initial emotional reaction has occurred, it is important to put things into perspective. Find a quiet place and a reflective mood. Then focus on yourself, your

child, your family, then the society or community in which you
live.

First, take a clear look at your own feelings to understand
and respond to what you can see going on inside you. No parent
is prepared to become the parent of a handicapped child. Be
honest and accepting of yourself. Realize what is normal and that
you are not superman or superwoman. You are, however, a loving
and capable child of God who has been given care of God's
special spirits to steward.

After you have dealt with some of your own feelings,
examine your handicapped child to see what is going on in his or
her life. A lot of your child's attitude cues will come directly from
you and the rest of the family. What are you directly and indi-
rectly telling him about his handicap?

Now take a close look at the whole family. As you feel success in parenting your handicapped child, you will find that good
parenting habits and concern can widen from primary interest in
the handicapped child and encompass the complete family
system.

Your horizons have now enlarged and you are able to make
more attempts to understand more clearly what is going on with
the community in relation to the handicapped. You will become
more familiar with day schools, volunteer agency programs,
special community outreach programs, special church programs, all for the handicapped and their families. Now you will
fully recognize that you are not alone in your quest to allow your
child as normal a life as possible.

Those are the general steps. Let's discuss more of the
specifics. An important step for all parents is to share the burdens as well as the blessings together. This is especially true for
a handicapped child. Many times the father does not seem to do
as much for the child as the mother, and the wife becomes bitter
that hubby isn't doing his share. Some husbands do dump a
handicap situation in their wife's lap, rationalizing with "It's the
mother's job to raise the children." This seems to be a copout on
the father's part and isn't conducive to successful child-rearing,
especially to raising a handicapped child.

Talk out this and any other related problems that may come
between your spouse and you. If these frustrated feelings
are kept bottled up, they fester and enlarge, becoming extremely
destructive. As you discuss a problem together it usually becomes less important and solutions seem to appear. The best
results come from mutual understanding and cooperation. So

talk out your problems with each other, with other parents who have similar problems, and with a professional worker if the need arises.

What we are really talking about is adjustment. The stories you have read are success stories because the handicapped persons and their families adjusted. A family is a constantly changing system. At first Mom and Dad make shifts in their lives as they come together in a new marriage. As a baby joins them, new adjustments are made. As the family grows, so do the adjustments, difficulties, good times, emotions and love! The family growing process is the same, even though one of the children is born with, or develops, a handicap. While it is true that certain unique difficulties must be faced, it is still a family system.

You will have to deal with some societal prejudice. Others outside the family system may complicate the situation by their reactions to your child. You cannot control to any great extent what others outside your family system think and feel. You can, however, combat that prejudice by building close relationships which tell all your children they are loveable and capable.

It is important to guard against the feelings that the ideal family system is commonplace. Be the family that you uniquely can be. Be strong, but not rigid. Be flexible, but not shallow. Be kind, but not soft. Positive discipline is the creator of successful family systems. Laughter and humor is an essential family ingredient. When Mom and Dad are happy and content, so usually are the children. Children zero in on the feelings of Mom and Dad. When you feel frustrated, so do they!

One protection against frustration is to talk together about the problem and not ignore or gloss over it. Handle first things first. One of the earliest considerations in planning a constructive program for the handicapped child is to get a diagnosis and a complete evaluation of his condition. The most successful way to do this is to put your faith in a professional team consisting of a physician, a psychologist, a social worker, and even an educational consultant. You can be a great help to this professional team by being realistic and not trying to overrate your child's ability. You then must accept the findings of the professional team before your child can really be helped.

Now you can concentrate on the development of the child. Healthy social relationships are created by the child feeling that he belongs and is accepted and loved. A feeling of security develops as he is able to successfully play with his siblings and other children. Social development is also a major factor and comes as he works, plays and learns to share with others. Physical development can reach its potential through play and work activities. Education is also essential, both at home and in programs adapted to the child's potentials.

As you work diligently to help your handicapped child reach his full potential, don't neglect the needs of the other family members, including your spouse. If the handicapped child's needs are always catered to first, the child may become self-centered and over-dependent. Other children may feel resentment. This may compound existing problems.

Include the complete family in discussions about family problems. An example may be that some handicapped children are disturbing to their brothers and sisters, and they feel uncomfortable about bringing friends home. If the children sense that the parents' attitude is comfortable toward *all* the children, it will be easier for the brothers and sisters to feel less embarrassment and include the handicapped child in their activities. Parents need to explain the handicap to their children and help them understand it. Others outside the family are bound to make comments and ask questions about "their retarded sister", etc. If the situation is talked about in the family, the children will feel free to help other people accept the handicapped member. It is important to understand, however, that no one child should expect to be included in *all* activities of the other children. Allow each child enough time for his or her own development. Mom and Dad shouldn't neglect the normal children and shower the handicapped child with too much love and attention in their presence. There will be conflicting feelings and resentment shown at certain times with the children and, if parents are observant, they can bring problems out in the open and allow everyone to talk about their feelings. Mom and Dad have their feelings and needs, too. You cannot give up your whole life for your handicapped child and expect to be a well-adjusted, self-respecting, contributing member of society.

Develop realistic goals for the whole family and for the handicapped child. Make sure everyone in the family knows what the goals are. When the goals are reached, celebrate and make a big issue of it. There will be successes and failures. Failures are a part of life, and you will probably learn more from your mistakes than your successes.

As the family system, including the handicapped child, functions, you will ask yourself many questions: Am I doing

enough? Am I doing too much? Am I too neglectful or too pro-
tective? Am I too soft, or maybe too firm? There are no general
answers to these questions. The best decisions are made using a
process such as the following:

1. Define the decision to be made.
2. Write down the existing alternatives you know about now.
3. List sources which may help you discover new alternatives.
4. Examine all the alternatives and choose the best one for
   all concerned.

Being calm, confident and in touch with your senses will
help you make the best decisions possible.

Sometimes decisions are not sharp and clear because we
cloud the issue by playing games. Eric Berne, in his classic
book, *The Games People Play*, suggests we all play games.
Handicapped children may have deadly serious games played
with them. An example would be a divorce, supposedly caused
by the handicapped child. While it is true that a handicapped
child in a family can cause greater pressures and problems (the
divorce rate among parents with retarded children is three times
the normal divorce rate), the real fact is that he is a scapegoat, an
excuse. The seeds of mistrust and dislike were already present. If
your family is strong and loving, a handicapped child won't break
it up.

Other games are also played. Some families may totally ignore the handicapped child and pretend he isn't really there and
not really one of the family. This stunts the development of the
child and the family. Some families go to the opposite extreme
and play the game of the handicapped child being super-human,
an "angel" on earth. This allows the handicapped child to be the
center of attention and control the family. The child develops a
very unrealistic view of the world and doesn't learn about real life.
He has to know that society won't cater to his every whim.

Some members of the family may also play the game of
blaming their own individual weaknesses and failures on the
handicapped child. Examples are: "I didn't get chosen to be a
cheerleader because my brother is retarded," or "I didn't get the
job advancement because the boss knows about our mongoloid
baby." This is also very destructive to the individual and the
family. There are many other games played which are an attempt
on the part of the person to avoid facing and solving his own
problems. Each family member accepting responsibility will
minimize these games. Your family needs to become aware of

any games they may be playing and talk it out in a family council openly and honestly.

These games and other problems may surface if professional counselors are utilized. If your family is successful in finding and following its own successful direction, a counselor may not be needed. If, however, that successful direction doesn't come, don't be afraid to use professional counselors. They may help you in many ways, such as:

1. Sharing physical burdens by helping secure admission to treatment facilities, school day camps, day care centers, etc.
2. Supplying "know-how" and "know-why".
3. Helping to secure financial assistance. Don't be afraid to use them when they are needed.

There are specific questions to be answered concerning the handicapped. One sensitive area is sexual development. Historically, we have shown a real fear and clumsiness in handling the sexuality of many handicapped children. Now we understand more, and recognize that growing and maturing involve risk to us all. Especially those who are mentally retarded must be helped to mature sexually in ways appropriate to their level of functioning. The groundwork is laid by parents who show tenderness, love and affection for each other. Then the delicate art of finding the most efficient balance of freedoms and limits in the developing life of the child needs to start early. A retarded adolescent will still have sexual desires, just like his normal brothers and sisters. Appropriate religious mores will need to guide him as they do the rest of the family. The key will be more time and patience.

A big question will be "What about marriage?" A handicapped person can find marriage a rich, rewarding experience or a tragedy, just like anyone else. His or her chances for a good marriage risk are dependent upon the following criteria:

1. Has he or she moved out of the early childhood stage of dependency?
2. Has he or she lived a successful, independent life for a time?
3. Has he or she shown, through independence, a drive to become creatively interdependent?
4. Does he or she show ability to assume responsibility? (Vital in the bearing and raising of children.)
5. Does he or she have the ability to love and understand the meaning of promise?

6. Does he or she have the ability to choose or give and take?

While this brief discussion is certainly oversimplified, it does give some direction. If the reader understands what makes sexual adjustment and a good marriage, he is then better able to help guide and direct all his children, the handicapped being no exception. Sex education is not a short course, but a lifelong journey that begins at birth. Parents are the ultimate teachers of sexuality, though professionals may be able to aid you. Crash courses on sexuality during adolescence is not the answer. Being sensitive, tender and confident with your child over a long period of time is.

Another far-reaching question to be dealt with is whether or not to institutionalize the handicapped child. Get professional counseling first. The degree of the handicap will swing the decision. Today the prevailing attitude is to keep the child home if the situation is manageable. If the handicap is so severe that twenty-four hour care is necessary, it may be too much of a strain on the family system. If, after much thought and prayer, your decision is to institutionalize, here are some considerations. Don't shy away from state schools just because of their name. Most are doing an excellent job in caring for the trainable and custodial child. The educable child (I.Q. from 50 to 75) will probably benefit more from living at home and going to a special school. For some children (not all), the institution provides good opportunity for quality of life. When choosing an institution, remember that a greater number of miles between you and your child usually causes a greater gap in your relationship. Close proximity is important if the child is to feel he or she is a family member in full standing. In summary, there is no way to simplify the fact of this decision being one of the hardest you will ever have to make.

Another question may be whether to try to keep your handicapped child in a special school setting, or in the usual school room situation. Be honest and realistic in your child's evaluation. Then decide what is best *for the child*. Some children have intelligence that is often average or better, but the individual can't succeed in academic pursuits. Included in this group is the physically handicapped child in whom intelligence is not easily assessed because his handicap renders him unable to perform tasks requested of him. Examples would be motor problems, such as cerebral palsy, congenital abnormalities, hearing and vision difficulties, etc.

Another concern many parents have is "what will happen to my handicapped child when we pass away?" "Should we try to keep him with us until death causes a separation?" Many handicapped persons can eventually become independent, productive members of society. Others may be able to become semi-independent or even live in a sheltered, small group living situation. You prepare for this day by programming the child's life as close as possible to the normal lifestyle of your other children. You do this by:

1. allowing him to take his fair share of risks
2. teaching him that success and failure is his responsibility
3. allowing him to experience more and bigger responsibilities
4. allowing him the chance to explore. He may have more capabilities than you think, and the more you protect him, the less he will learn to live in the outside world.

You can be helped with these points today by more complete and professional community-based services. Know what these services are and become involved in developing and bettering community services for the handicapped.

Do everything you can to allow your child the opportunity to experience human dignity. If you don't fully understand this statement, then ask yourself, "What makes me human?" Your child should have that same experience. By fighting to allow your child to have as normal and full a life as possible, your own life will be more rewarding. No one has asked you to sacrifice your life for the child. It doesn't seem that God meant it to be that way.

Summary

Parenting a handicapped child does have both its difficult and its rewarding times. Many times goal aspirations and role demands are different. The old "go home and treat him like a normal child" is so easy to say and so hard to do, yet vitally necessary. The following points summarize the main ideas of this chapter:

1. We live in an imperfect world, and defects are part of it. A defective baby can be born to virtually any set of parents.
2. Be familiar with normal patterns of physical, emotional and intellectual growth. If you notice abnormal development, have your child professionally evaluated by a team. They will integrate their findings to give a truer pic-

ture. A great deal of shopping around from one specialist to another is ineffective and uncoordinated.

3. If a handicap is involved, straighten out your own thinking so you can realistically accept the situation. Accept that your child is very human and has the same basic needs as you and your other children.
4. Make the handicapped child an essential part of the whole family system.
5. Become involved in local and national programs. This helps you see your problems in better perspective. You rub shoulders with other parents who have similar concerns. Care and treatment facilities become more available to you.

Every set of parents, whether or not they have a handicapped child, has unique problems. The "perfect family" is probably not an earthly reality. Your stewardship as parents is to help each child and yourselves to reach their full potential.

Chapter 21

A Religious Look at the Handicapped

The key to being a successful parent, of either a handicapped or a normal child, is to know the purpose of life itself. The purpose of life is tied to the religious experience of man. The religious understanding of handicaps has changed drastically from early man to our generation.

In Biblical times, it was believed that those who had crippled bodies and minds had evil spirits or were demon-controlled. Medieval Europe regarded the mentally retarded as "changlings." It was believed that quasi-humans replaced the human infant from its bed with one of its own.

Even medical writings of the nineteenth and early twentieth centuries discussed handicaps as evolving from "bad blood" or similar innuendos referred to as "the sins of the father." Scientific study has helped us to regard these beliefs as being ignorant and frustrated attempts to explain the unknown. Some people still hang onto these old ideas tenaciously.

Writers from our own time show an extreme attitude change. In the early 1950's Dale Evans Rogers wrote about her own mongoloid child in her book, *Angel Unaware*. She referred to her handicapped child as a special messenger sent from God. Others also refer to the handicapped as God's children, with some implication that these special people are not fully human and are above humanity, so they must be Gods.

This attitude shift is certainly a better and more realistic view than earlier, but it still denies that the handicapped are like us— the supposed normal human beings. New attitudes are showing more acceptance with the idea that handicapped children are "more like us than different from us." Many religions now teach that all humans have strengths as well as limitations, and each human must make a life according to his own uniqueness.

This philosophy was very apparent in a study conducted by the writers during 1975-76. Each of the Catholic, Protestant, and Latter-day Saint religions were questioned regarding their theological beliefs concerning the handicapped.

The responses of the various religions were very revealing. The LDS viewpoint is discussed after the other religions express their views.

Our first question dealt with how the handicapped children fit into the plan of God. A common response was that God is the ultimate origin of all life, and therefore every creature comes into his world by the act of his creating love. Every child, from his earliest development fits in, in some way, in God's plan. God has a plan for the life of everyone, no matter what stage of development they are in. A strong Protestant feeling was that:

> God is uniquely concerned about the general welfare of all mentally and physically handicapped children. His great compassion abounds toward them. They have a special place in His eternal affections. His divine will in time and eternity is to compensate them in glorious ways.
>
> They deserve respect as all other humans and are expected to participate in life as they are able. Their spiritual accountability is also as they have potential, and as infants are eternally secure and included in Christ's redemption as innocent ones.

The Roman Catholic faith had a similar comment, which was expressed in a personal letter to the author. "Jesus Christ died for all men including the handicapped. First: to make an atonement for their sins. Secondly: for the healing of their bodies and mind." (Isaiah 53:4-5, 1 Peter 2:24, Matthew 8:17)

A common teaching throughout the responses explained that "mentally handicapped children and people who are morally not accountable are considered as innocent in the sight of God because they are covered by the redemption offered by Christ, the same as little children."

Parents of a handicapped child have a responsibility to develop love and care for that child; thus he becomes a blessing to the parents and helps them to reflect the love and the care of God and thus become more godlike. They are to accept the child as a gift from God, upon whom mercy, grace, and love from God may be bestowed on the child through the parents' love to God. The parents have an opportunity to be an instrument used by God for the child's salvation and welfare.

They need to be supported in their added responsibilities. They should be fully accepted like all other parents and in no way made to feel guilty or of second-rate character.

Parents should develop positive outlooks on life. Even if their offspring have congenital defects, parents should never harbor feelings of guilt. Their duty and sacred privilege is to aid handicapped youngsters in their care to develop whatever creative potential the children have.

Parents should prove able to see through the pain of having a handicapped child the opportunity for a glorious personal improvement of their moral personalities.

Among the general truths in this area, however, Scripture indicates that in some cases children suffer because of the sins of their parents (Exodus 20:5) while in other cases sin is not the cause. (John 9:3).

If a child is handicapped because of the sin of his parents, there is forgiveness for those who have sinned (1 John 1:9). While forgiveness is certain for those who ask God for it, unfortunately there are some penalties for sin which the grace of God does not eliminate in this life. For instance, if a child is born to parents with venereal disease, God will forgive the parents, but the child may suffer all its life because of the parents' past sins.

Concerned parents of handicapped children need special help in distinguishing between cases where they were at fault and where they were not; between cases resulting from deliberate acts and acts of innocence or accident. If the problem exists because of sin, God will enable the parent(s) to know this immediately, and grant forgiveness as soon as it is requested (1 John 3:20). If there is not an immediate awareness that the handicap exists because of sin, the parents should not continue to seek for a reason. Rather they should recognize that God has permitted a situation to happen as in the case of Job's suffering, and that He has a way of making all things work together for good to them that love Him (Romans 8:28).

Our second probe asked if the handicapped would experience any eternal handicap. Every religion answered an emphatic *no!* There is an earthly body and there is a heavenly body. (II Corinthians 5:1-4). Everything Heaven provides is perfect, therefore there are no handicapped bodies or minds in Heaven.

We know definitely that children will not be eternally handicapped (1 Corinthians 15:42-44). To illustrate this Paul uses an agricultural figure (1 Corinthians 15:37,38). A seed such as a kernel of corn may be terribly marred, but when it is planted it provides perfect kernels of corn. This figure illustrates the transformation believing handicapped people will enjoy in the afterlife.

Others commented that the handicapped would not experience their physical or mental burden after this life because their present handicap is of this earth and is a part of what is considered the fall of man and sin on the earth. When the Lord Jesus Christ returns and the earth is redeemed and renewed, there will be no such thing as an eternal handicap. Therefore, no physical infirmities can affect the eternal soul but only insofar as the handicapped person will allow.

Several of the religions referred to Isaiah 35:6—"Then shall the lame man leap as an hart, and the tongue of the dumb sing; for in the wilderness shall waters break out, and streams in the desert." We believe that this verse refers to the immortal state of man in the earth made new.

When then asked "Do they have a special mission here on earth?," almost all replied "Yes!" We all have a special mission. God has placed each individual person in the world for a purpose, and this includes the handicapped. "A handicapped person can ultimately prove to have a special mission, principally within his own immediate environment. Their potential to achieve indeed is very limited, but God can use their handicap to teach the rest of us patience, helpfulness, love, gratitude, respect for life."

A common question asked through the ages concerns the parents of the handicapped child, and have they done some wrong to receive this child. Many referred to St. John 9:1-5. "When a handicapped person was brought to Jesus, he was asked whether this man had sinned or his parents. Jesus made it very clear that neither was the case; that is, handicaps are not the result or punishment of sins."

Common threads weaved into the following philosophy.

Whether or not the cause of the handicap is known, parents should pray for the healing of the child (2 Samuel 12:16; Mark 5:23). There are times when God in His sovereign wisdom heals in answer to prayer. There are also times when God does not heal the sick. This is another one of the areas where God has not given us all the answers.

The parents of a handicapped child are still to continue the responsibility of parenthood and to endeavor to understand their child as to his degree of handicap and see to it that this child is given every opportunity to develop to the limit of his capacity. Certainly the love of parents can cover the deficiencies of a handicapped child.

Has God purposefully sent this child to them? Some religions answered that they didn't think so. Natural causes explain these conditions. However when such disabilities confront a family, its members have opportunity to react in constructive ways which are means to worthwhile ends in growth of children and parents.

God proportions to each individual the grace which he needs in order to face a difficult situation. God does not delight or purposely bring about deformity or underdevelopment in any of his creatures.

Others suggested that God allows it to happen but does not purposefully send such a child. One religion stated that God purposely sends every child to its parents.

To pursue the above question we asked "Is the birth of a handicapped child just a law of nature?" The idea of the imperfect world we live in is brought out forcefully.

In the fall of man the scar, blight, degradation of sin of the human race on earth brings the possibility of deformity in all forms of life. Sometimes a child is born handicapped due to abuse of health by its mother while the child is in its prenatal state. This would, wittingly or unwittingly, be the result of maternal action.

Deformity or underdevelopment is a law of nature only as a result of the tragedy of sin that has infected our world.

God is the ultimate author of everything that transpires in this world. He has made the laws of nature and he uses them for his purposes.

Laws of cause and effect are constantly in operation. Causes which activate these effects sometimes go back several generations. Similarly, our current actions, yours and mine, can affect people henceforth for better or for worse.

Finally, we questioned whether a handicapped child is a blessing or a burden in a family, or both. The statements that flow from the various religions are presented in their original form for clarity.

It would seem that whether the handicapped child is a burden or a blessing depends on the attitude of the family. Scripture indicates that the mentally handicapped should have special consideration (1 Thessalonians 5:14). Our position is that those people who live according to the teaching of Scripture will be the best adjusted parents. In addition to the spiritual and mental health they enjoy, they can also expect the special help of a loving Heavenly Father to cope with the difficult situations of life.

We believe that parents should first make their peace with God by accepting Jesus Christ as Savior and Lord (John 3:16-19; Romans 10:9-10). After this, they have the assurance that God will allow nothing to come their way which is greater than they can handle (1 Corinthians 10:13).

Any handicap can be a source of personal and spiritual and mental growth on the part of parents and family. That has happened many times. In other situations handicapped children were considered just a burden.

The experience of raising handicapped children can be a blessing if the parents can use the opportunity for greater accomplishment of patience. The greater "burdens" that are overcome in this life would have a greater intensity of fulfillment. A "handicapped" child in the family should never be used as an excuse for one's own weak behavior and development.

A handicapped child can prove a salvation to a family or the cause of its moral deterioration and final dissolution. It depends on the parents.

Many handicapped children occasion serious problems at times. Thus, they may be deemed burdens. (But don't so-called normal children also cause difficulties?) Handicapped children unquestionably are affectionate and often helpful in small ways. They are immense blessings.

Of course it depends a great deal on the extent of the child's condition and the attitude of the family. They can be both a blessing and a burden and seldom only one of these.

Yes, a handicapped child can definitely be a blessing in the family. Many families with handicapped children have given thanks for their presence. This does not mean that such children do not present burdens. There are burdens and responsibilities with all of life.

Of course, handicapped children can be a blessing in the family. In one sense, every child is a burden, but love makes that burden light and joyous. This can be just as true in the situation of a handicapped child as it can with a normal child.

A child can be a blessing to a family so that God's love, mercy, and grace can be activated through the parents. It may become a burden if the parents fail to see God's purpose and plan in sending them the child.

The Latter-day Saint (Mormon) viewpoint on the handicapped is somewhat similar, and yet in some aspects distinct from that of other Christian religions. It's views are heavily enmasked in the purpose of life as Mormons understand it.

The Latter-day Saint religion gives a meaningful explanation of man's mission in life and of the necessary development of one's character in a world where courage and sacrifice are required. We are told that to bring about the perfection of our souls, it is necessary—while in our mortal existence on earth—to come in contact with pain, temptation and sorrow. In the world of spirits we cannot suffer physical pain, nor can we fully understand the things that happen only in mortal life. We have to experience them here in order to have this knowledge and thus complete our plan of salvation. We are told that we were informed that we would have to suffer the ills of mortality, that we would be tried and tested. Knowing this, we still chose to come.

The parents who have the opportunity of the special child in their home often have great things required of them. It is commonly experienced among these parents that great trials also bring great blessings when attitudes are right.

Mary V. Hill enlarges upon this idea:

> Someday we may well find that these trials are in reality among the greatest of blessings, though now they appear to us as blessings in disguise. [1]

President Spencer W. Kimball of the LDS church sums up the Mormon theological viewpoint on handicaps as he discusses abortion.

---

[1] Hill, Mary V., *Angel Children* (Bountiful, Utah: Horizon Publishers, 1973), pg. 44.

Let us consider the question of abortion in cases of possible defective babies. No one, save the Lord himself, has the right to decide if a baby should or should not be permitted to life. All human life is sacred. One of life's most Christian opportunities is to work with those who have handicaps. And while handicaps are a part of the imperfect world in which we now live, in the resurrection there will be no blind eyes, no deaf ears, and no crippled legs. In eternity there will be no retarded minds, no diseased or injured bodies. In the eternal perspective, such infirmities exist but for a moment, yet some people would play the part of God and deny mortality to helpless children within the womb. And many that were thought to be afflicted will be born without blemish. [2]

The Book of Mormon, accepted by Latter-day Saints as the word of God, comments on those who specifically have mental retardation handicaps, stating that:

...all little children are alive in Christ and also they that are without the law.   (Moroni 8:2)

This important scripture is enlarged upon by Elder Bruce R. McConkie, a Latter-day Saint General Authority, as he states:

Obviously, if children or adults do not develop mentally to the point where they know right from wrong and have the normal intellect of an accountable person, they never arrive at the years of accountability no matter how many actual years they may live. Such persons, though they may be adults, are without the law, cannot repent, are under no condemnation. [3]

Joseph Fielding Smith, a former LDS Church President, also expounded upon this subject in his important work, *Doctrines of Salvation:*

---

[2] Kimball, Spencer W., "The Right to Live," a tape recording (Salt Lake City, Utah: The Church of Jesus Christ of Latter-day Saints, 1975.)

[3] McConkie, Bruce R., *Mormon Doctrine* (Salt Lake City, Utah: Bookcraft, Inc., 1966), pg. 853

For those who are mentally deficient, through no fault of their own, someday these pressures will be lifted—so that there will be no limit to the possibilities of their spirits, their minds, and their souls.

Little children who die before they reach the years of accountability will automatically inherit the celestial kingdom. All we need do for children is to have them sealed to their parents. They need no baptism and never will, for our Lord has performed all the work necessary for them. So far as the ordinance of sealing (marriage) is concerned, this may wait until the millenium. [4]

This background information leads us to the response given by Terry J. Mayer of the LDS Welfare Services Division. His answers to our questions, though not an official statement of the LDS church, gives excellent insight into LDS philosophy:

1. How do the handicapped fit into the plan of God:
Handicapped individuals have perfect spirits. The infirmities of their bodies are the temporary results of natural processes of cause and effect in an imperfect world. "For it must needs be, that there is an opposition in all things."

(Book of Mormon, 2 Nephi 2:11)

2. Will they be eternally handicapped?
"The soul shall be restored to the body, and the body to the soul; yea, and every limb and joint shall be restored to its body; yea, even a hair of the head shall not be lost; but all things shall be restored to their proper and perfect frame."

(Book of Mormon, Alma 40:23)

3. What is your philosophy concerning the parents of a handicapped child?
The parents of a handicapped child have special opportunities to grow in terms of love, service, and patience.

The Savior, when asked whether one man's blindness from birth was a punishment for the man's or the man's parents' sin, replied "neither hath this man sinned, nor his parents; but that the works of God should be made manifest in him."

(John 9:1-3)

---

[4] McConkie, Bruce R. [comp.], *Doctrines of Salvation* (Salt Lake City, Utah: Bookcraft, Inc., 1954), Vol. II, pp. 54,55.

4. Has God purposefully sent this child to them?

God has purposefully sent this spirit to them, but did not necessarily cause nor desire that the physical body be handicapped.

"Therefore, let your hearts be comforted; for all things shall work together for good to them that walk uprightly, and to the sanctification of the Church."

(Doctrine and Covenants 100:15)

5. Is the birth of a handicapped child just a law of nature?

There are some spirit children of our Heavenly Father whose eternal progression would best be fostered through life in a handicapped body. Likewise, there will be some parents who will grow tremendously in such a context. That all-knowing Parent of us all who numbers even the sparrows knows and loves each of us, and uses the laws of nature to achieve His eternal purposes.

6. Can a handicapped child be a blessing in a family? or just a burden? or both?

A handicapped child may very well be a great blessing to a family by being a burden. It is solving problems, mastering weaknesses, coping with difficulties that we learn and grow and progress toward perfection.

"...fear not, let your hearts be comforted; yea, rejoice evermore, and in everything give thanks."

(Doctrine and Covenants 98:1)

Birth is not the beginning, nor death the ending of our existence. Each of us lived before earth life, the literal spirit offspring of our Heavenly Father. Following death, our spirits (and ultimately, our bodies) live still. Mortality is but a moment in man's eternal journey. The afflictions and infirmities of earth life result from the natural causes and effects of the imperfect world in which we live.

God has said: "Be patient in afflictions, for thou shalt have many; but endure them, for, lo, I am with thee, even unto the end of thy days."

(Doctrine and Covenants 24:8)

And again, "For my thoughts are not your thoughts, neither are your ways my ways, saith the Lord. For as the heavens are higher than the earth, so are my ways higher than your ways, and my thoughts than your thoughts."

(Isaiah 55:8-9)

It has been said that perhaps God has allowed adversity in the world to foster courage; sickness to employ service; sorrow to build faith; weakness to gain strength. He has said: I give unto men weakness that they may be humble—for if they humble themselves before me and have faith in me, *then will I make weak things become strong* unto them." (B. of M., Ether 12:27)

By understanding that there is a purpose for our trials, and by sharing the burdens of those trials with our fellowman, we may find strength in the assurance that something good can be gained from something bad.

We also may take comfort in the words of the Lord, when he said: "...know thou, my son, that all these things shall give thee experience, and be for thy good. The Son of Man hath descended below them all. Art thou greater than He? Therefore, hold on thy way..." (Doctrine and Covenants 122:7-9)

Appendix

Resources for Working with the Handicapped

Abraham Lincoln was once asked a question that many parents of handicapped and normal children ask themselves. "What do you do when you come to the end of your rope?"

Mr. Lincoln replied, "Tie a knot in it and hang on!"

Parents may ask themselves this question many times. Some often feel that no one cares, that they, who need the most consideration, seem to receive the least. Parents of handicapped children in particular may suffer guilt, anxiety, frustration, tension, anger, weariness, and impatience.

It is important for parents to recognize that there is help. There are many private and public agencies whose work it is to fulfill the educational, medical, and recreational needs of handicapped children.

Some of the community resources include visiting nurse services, homemaker and home health aid services, speech therapists, outpatient services of medical and dental schools, and university health services. There are the State Crippled Children's programs which offer free or low-cost diagnostic services, and the many voluntary health associations. Some programs, such as the National Institute for Health (an agency of HEW) are not directly involved with health services but do a great deal of research to aid the handicapped.

Treatment programs for the handicapped have changed considerably. In primitive societies the handicapped were hidden in the home or left to exposure with resultant death. Western society would institutionalize the handicapped as soon as possible. Now we understand that institutionalization, especially in infancy, may have a handicapping effect on the mental and social development of the child. The emphasis today is to provide special facilities for the education and treatment of handicapped children in our own communities so they can remain at home as long as possible.

With these ideas in mind, the following comprehensive list of "help" agencies are presented as a resource to the parents who may need them. When contacting these sources of help, it is helpful to be as specific as possible about what is requested and to briefly describe the person involved and the problem for which help is being sought.

The sources of help are listed in alphabetical order under the defect or handicap with information on some of the sources.

1. Allergies

An allergy is an abnormal and individual hypersensitivity to substances (plant pollen, bee toxin) that are ordinarily harmless. Allergies most commonly affect the respiratory passages and the skin, but other body organs and systems may be affected. An allergy can be severe enough to be handicapping to the individual involved (e.g., asthma). An official organization which conducts research and conducts education programs concerning allergies is the:

Allergy Foundation of America
801 Second Avenue
New York, NY 10017

2. Arthritis

This term covers more than 100 different types of joint diseases, but basically means inflammation of a joint. It is quite rare among those under the age of 25, but does occur and can be very crippling. More information on specific arthritic conditions and treatments can be obtained from:

The Arthritis Foundation
1212 Avenue of the Americas
New York, NY 10036

3. Autism

This condition involves the psyche, and is characterized by extreme withdrawal and failure to relate to other persons. The autistic child responds chiefly to his environment. He may appear immature and mentally retarded. Some children may be partially autistic. Progress is being made in the treatment of autism and more specific information and help can be procured from the:

National Society for Autistic Children
621 Central Avenue
Albany, NY 12206

4. Blindness

Blindness, the inability to see, is legally defined as having less than 20/200 vision with eyeglasses or contact lenses. (A person with 20/200 vision is able to see at 20 feet what the normal eye can see at 200 feet.) Much of the blindness caused in newborn children has been eliminated through the use of silver nitrate and more careful administration of oxygen after birth. Heredity, infectious diseases and congenital problems (e.g., rubella or German measles) still cause some blindness, as do accidents. New methods of education and recreation are helping the blind immensely. The following organizations can provide information and help:

American Foundation for the Blind, Inc.
15 West 16th Street
New York, NY 10011

Association for Education of the Visually Handicapped
1604 Spruce Street
Philadelphia, PA 19103

Association for the Visually Handicapped
1839 Frankfort Avenue
Louisville, KY 40206

National Aid to the Visually Handicapped
3201 Balboa Street
San Francisco, CA 94121

National Society for Prevention of Blindness, Inc.
79 Madison Avenue
New York, NY 10016

Library of Congress
Division for the Blind and Physically Handicapped
Washington, D.C 20542

This organization offers free library services for the visually and physically handicapped).

5. Cancer

Cancer is a neoplastic disease in which there is an unregulated growth of abnormal cells. These abnormal cells continue to reproduce until they form a mass of tissue known as a tumor. There are many types of cancers. The most common type of children's cancer is leukemia, a cancer of the tissues in the bone marrow, spleen, and lymph nodes. The white blood cells rapidly reproduce, causing a reduction of red blood cells to produce anemia and increased susceptibility to infection and hemorrhage. An early diagnosis of any type of cancer is the key. Treatments can be of great benefit. More information on causes and treatment can be received from the:

American Cancer Society
219 East 42nd Street
New York, NY 10017

Leukemia Society of America, Inc.
211 East 43rd Street
New York, NY 10017

6. Crippled Children

This isn't a specific classification, because "crippled" signifies the end result of many maladies ranging from accidents in cars, etc., to polio and other crippling diseases. There are organizations, however, who deal with a wide range of crippling problems, such as:

The National Foundation—March of Dimes
P.O. Box 2000
White Plains, NY 10602

(This organization did work with polio victims. More recently it also specializes in birth defects and educates with pamphlets on birth defects, drugs, Rh factor, rubella, filmstrips, family medical records, lists of genetic counseling centers, and medical services).

Association for the Aid of Crippled Children
345 East 46th Street
New York, NY 10017
(Specifically gives information on Spina bifida)

National Easter Seal Foundation for Crippled Children and Adults
2023 W. Ogden Avenue
Chicago, IL 60612

7. Cystic Fibrosis

Cystic fibrosis is a chronic, noncontagious, hereditary disease which affects about one baby in every 1000 in the U.S. It is the basic cause of a large percentage of chronic lung disease among children

Cystic fibrosis is caused by the lack of one enzyme, which results in metabolic error in the body, particularly in the exocrine glands. A child with cystic fibrosis has a heavy production of sticky mucous in the lungs and pancreas. Lung infections are easily developed and the digestion of food in the intestines is interfered with. Perspiration contains a very high concentration of salt.

In recent years, better methods of diagnosis and treatment have considerably lengthened the life expectancy of C.F. children. The organization to contact for information on literature, treatment, and financial aids for cystic fibrosis children is:

National Cystic Fibrosis Research Foundation
3379 Peachtree Road N.E.
Atlanta, GA 30326

8. Deafness

Deafness is impairment of hearing. Total deafness is quite rare, but partial deafness is common with approximately 15 million Americans experiencing some degree of deafness. About 2.5 million of these are children whose deafness is congenital (from birth) or developed before the age of five.

The two major types of deafness are conductive (interruption of sound vibrations to the inner ear) and sensorineural (interruption of sound interpretation in the nerves or brain). One of the most common causes of congenital deafness is viral infections, particularly rubella, contracted by the mother during pregnancy.

Medical science has made great progress in the treatment of conditions which cause deafness. Drugs and microsurgery are two of the greatest areas of progress. For information and help regarding deafness, the following organizations should be contacted:

American Hearing Society, or
National Association of Hearing and Speech Agencies
919 18th Street, N.W.
Washington, D.C. 20006
(The services offered by this organization include lip-reading classes, rehabilitation, and hearing aid clinics).

American Speech and Hearing Association
1001 Connecticut Avenue N.W.
Washington, D.C. 20006
(This is a professional association of specialists in speech and hearing therapy).

Alexander Graham Bell Association for the Deaf, Inc.
The Volta Bureau for the Deaf
3417 Volta Place, N.W.
Washington, D.C. 20007
(This organization operates one of the world's finest libraries on deafness, and functions as a deafness information center).

Deafness Research Foundation
366 Madison Avenue
New York, NY 10017
(Conducts medical research into the causes of deafness).

National Association of the Deaf
905 Bonifant Street
Silver Springs, MD

John Tracy Clinic
807 W. Adams Blvd.
Los Angeles, CA 90007
(Conducts education for deaf children)

9. Diabetes

Though there are different types of diabetes (bronze, insipidus, and mellitus), the most common type is diabetes mellitus. This is a disorder of carbohydrate metabolism in which the ability to oxidize and utilize carbohydrates is lost as a result of problems connected with the normal insulin mechanism. This, in turn, leads to abnormalities of protein and fat metabolism. The main factor lies in the decrease of quality or quantity of insulin from the islands of Langerhans in the pancreas. This causes the diabetic to be improperly nourished. Unused glucose accumulates and spills over to the urine, leaving the diabetic weak and fatigued. Other body organs, such as blood vessels, hands and feet, heart, kidneys, nervous system, and the eyes may eventually be affected.

Treatment of diabetes depends on the age of the diabetic, the symptoms shown, and the severity of the disease. Though there is no cure, the disease can be controlled by exercise, diet, and insulin administration. More information and help on the disease and its control can be received from the:

American Diabetes Association
18 East 48th Street
New York, NY 10017

(This organization will send out special booklets which instruct the diabetic and his family)

10. Dwarfism [Short stature]

This category includes achondroplasia and hypopituitarism. Today, people who experience these types of birth defects are called, and call themselves, the "Little People."

Though there are different types of short stature, the causative factor is usually chromosomal errors. Midgets are normally proportioned individuals of short stature, caused usually by hypopituitarism. This term refers to a lack of normal functioning of the pituitary gland.

A dwarf is an unusually short person whose body usually has a slightly enlarged head and usually short and stocky arms and legs. The most common form of dwarfism is achondroplasia. This is a genetic condition caused by a gene mutation. There are also other types of dwarfs. A professional medical evaluation is important to the future of the child and the decision of the parents to have more children. The chances of the specific disorders to occur again in the same family differ. The following organizations will be helpful:

Little People of America, Inc.
P.O. Box 126
Owatonna, Minnesota 55060

The National Genetics Foundations
250 West 57th Street
New York, NY 10019

11. Epilepsy

Epilepsy is a disorder of the nervous system in which the major symptom is a convulsive seizure, which is the result of a temporary disturbance of the brain impulses. It is the most common organic disorder of the nervous system, with over 1,860,000 Americans being affected by it.

There are different types of epilepsy such as petit mal, grand mal, jacksonian, and psychomotor. The intensity and type of loss of consciousness and involuntary convulsive movements differ for each one. The causes of epilepsy are varied, but are usually physical causes such as injury to the brain at birth, brain tumor or a wound or blow to the head. The treatment for controlling the seizures can be very successful. Anticonvulsant drugs (e.g., phenobarbitol) are usually used. The following organization supplies information on all aspects of epilepsy, and can refer epileptic victims to clinics and specialists in their locality:

Epilepsy Foundation of America
1828 "L" Street, N.W.
Suite 406
Washington, D.C. 20036

12. General Categories

Certain organizations are general in nature and can help in a wide variety of situations. They are:

American Academy of Pediatrics
1801 Hinman Avenue
Evanston, IL 60204
(Specializes in all aspects of child care)

American Association for Maternal and Child Health
116 S. Michigan Avenue
Chicago, IL 60603
(Concerned with the prevention of birth defects and proper care of the child)

American Medical Asociation
535 N. Dearborn Street
Chicago, IL 60610
(Concerned with all aspects of child care)

National Clearinghouse for Drug Abuse Information (NIMH)
5600 Fishers Lane
Rockville, MD 20852

National Tuberculosis and Respiratory Disease Association
1740 Broadway
New York, NY 10019

Boy Scouts of America
North Brunswick, New Jersey 08902
(Scouting information for children with handicaps)

Closer Look
Box 19428
Washington, D.C. 20036

(A national Special Education Information Center designed to help parents and those concerned find services and help for children with physical, mental, emotional, and learning handicaps. This organization is sponsored by the U.S. Department of Health, Education, and Welfare)

U.S. Public Health Service
National Institutes of Health
Public Information Officer
Bethesda, Maryland 20014
(This organization will send information about specific birth defects)

The Medic Alert Foundation International
1000 North Palm
Turlock, California 95380
(This organization provides individual indentification of specific problems that a person can have on his person, such as a card or bracelet)

13. **Heart Diseases**
The most common handicapping heart disorders among children and young adults are congenital heart defects. There are appoximately 35 kinds of congenital defects, with about 20 kinds being partially or completely cured by surgery. A little more than one percent of American babies experience a congenital heart or blood vessel defect.

Causes range from viral infections (rubella, Coxsackie) to the mother while pregnant to an environmental condition during pregnancy, such as drugs and radiation. There is some evidence that heart defects have a family basis.

An early diagnosis is the key to treatment. X-rays, blood tests, an electrocardiogram, angiocardiography, are all diag-

nostic measures. The most effective treatment is surgery. More information on heart disorders can be received from the:
American Heart Association
44 East 23rd Street
New York, NY 10010

14. Hemophilia

Hemophilia is a condition characterized by impaired coagulability (the blood won't clot) of the blood, and a strong tendency to bleed when blood vessels are interfered with. This disease is heredity (inherited) and limited mainly to males. Spontaneous hemorrhage (bleeding) and stiff joints can lead to permanent crippling if it is untreated.

Hemophiliacs can be educated to avoid trauma and obtain prompt medical attention for any bleeding. When bleeding does occur, the clotting factor level in the blood is raised and blood transfusions are given. For more information, write to:
The National Hemophilia Foundation
25 West 39th Street
New York, NY 10018

15. Huntington's Chorea

This is a rare hereditary disease of the brain, and is characterized by spastic, involuntary muscle movements, mental deterioration and speech disturbances. The disease shows up in adulthood (30-45 years of age). The condition gradually (15 or so years) incapacitates the victim until he finally dies. There is no known cure, and treatment will only give temporary relief of the symptoms. The organization to contact is the:
Committee to Combat Huntington's Disease
200 W. 57th Street
New York, NY 10019

16. Kidney Disorders

The kidneys are the filtering system in the body. A disabled kidney is extremely crippling. Kidney disorders include inflammation, infection, structural defects, obstructions, injuries, tumors, and calculus formation. Kidney problems are rare in children, but they can occur. More understanding of kidney problems, diagnosis, and treatment can be obtained from the:
National Kidney Foundation
116 East 17th Street
New York, NY 10010

17. Learning Disabilities [due to minimal brain dysfunction]

In the past, many terms have been used to describe what medical science now calls minimal brain dysfunction. These include hyperactivity, agressive behavior disorder, hyperkinetic impulse disorder, character disorder, aphasia, neurophrenia, psychoneurological learning disorder, dyslexia, perceptual handicap, organic brain damage, and association deficit pathology.

It has been estimated that as many as 15 to 20 percent of American school children suffer from some degree of behavior and learning disabilities caused by minimal brain dysfunction. For some reason, the boys outnumber the girls 6 or 10 to 1. The causes are varied, including heredity, congenital malformation, and almost anything that can affect the central nervous system before or during birth, or in early childhood. Difficult and long births, prematurity, and inborn metabolic errors are all suspect. There have been hundreds of different symptoms described of minimal brain dysfunction, but they can be put into a few categories:

1. Abnormal activity—such as overly-active, restless, can't sit still. Speech comes in disorganized torrents, and sleep is easily disrupted.

2. Impulsiveness—the child acts or talks before he thinks. He is easily distracted and is described as explosive, uninhibited, and reckless.

3. Short attention span—he has trouble concentrating on any one thing, and any movement seems to distract him.

4. Poor coordination—he has trouble making his eyes and hands work together smoothly.

5. Emotional instability—exploding rage will be provoked by slight frustrations. He panics easily, is quick tempered, and has a hard time playing with more than one child at a time.

6. Immature development—he tends to look and act young for his age and shows nervous habits.

7. Perceptual disabilities—he has trouble perceiving distance and depth, and may not see or hear what other people do.

8. Specific learning disabilities—he may achieve well in one area but do very poorly in another.

9. Language disorders—speech development may be slow with stuttering experienced. Difficulty in understanding directions and mispronounced words or sounds are common.

10. Neurological signs—he may exhibit certain neurological abnormalities, such as "different" reflexes, and focusing difficulties with his eyes.

This list could go on and on. The prime consideration is for an early diagnosis by a medical team. This saves the parents from blaming themselves that they have ruined the child, and it causes the child to receive needed help before he develops permanent psychological scars and labeling.

There is no certain method of treatment, but certain drugs and individually tailored educational programs help considerably. A family who builds the child's self-concept is a key factor. The following organizations can help immensely:

Association for Children with Learning Disabilities
2200 Brownsville Road
Pittsburgh, Pennsylvania 15210

Council for Exceptional Children
1411 Jefferson Davis Highway
Arlington, Virginia 22202
(A department of the National Education Association)

18. **Mental Retardation**

Mental retardation is a faulty or inadequate development of the brain which causes some degree of inability to learn and adapt to normal life. This may be caused before, during, or after birth, by infections, radiation, accidents, drugs, malformations such as hydrocephalus, and chemical abnormalities. Children may experience mental retardation from an impoverished environment, such as lack of mental stimulation, poor family relationships, or a non-nourishing culture and society. It is important to regard mental retardation as a general term for a wide range of conditions, and is not a disease.

Mental retardation is a relative term, with its meaning depending upon what society demands of the person in social responsibility, skills, and learning. The range of mental retardation is wide, with the slightest being severe enough to prevent a child from functioning effectively with his peers. Medical science uses a measurement of I.Q. below 70, but I.Q. is only a rough measurement and can change.

It is estimated in the U.S. that approximately 3-5 million persons have subnormal intelligence. An early diagnosis will allow the child to benefit from special education and training which can lead to greater independence. Some potentially retarding diseases, such as P.K.U. and meningitis, can be treated successfully to prevent any retardation. Some types of potential mental retardation situations can be prevented by wise decision-making by the mother (e.g., syphilis). Education and help from experts can make the difference. Contact these organizations for both.

American Association on Mental Deficiency
5201 Connecticut Avenue, N.W.
Washington, D.C.

The Children's Bureau
U.S. Department of Health, Education, and Welfare
Washington, D.C. 20201
(Supplies information on schools and other facilities for retarded children)

Joseph P. Kennedy, Jr. Foundation
Suite 205, 1701 "K" Street, N.W.
Washington, D.C. 20002

National Association for Retarded Children
2709 Avenue "E"
East Arlington, Texas 76011
(Supplies information on the facilities that are available in any local area)

The National Associations for Mental Health
1800 North Kent Street
Rosslyn Station
Arlington, Virginia 22209

19. Neuromuscular Problems

The word neuromuscular pertains to the nerves and muscles of the body. Included in this category are the handicapping disorders that affect the nervous and muscular systems, such as cerebral palsy, muscular dystrophy, multiple sclerosis, paraplegia, and Tay-Sachs disease.

Cerebral palsy is a partial paralysis and lack of muscle coordination resulting from a birth defect, disease or injury of the brain tissue. These defects are usually caused at or near the time of birth and can be due to premature birth, blood type incompatability, lack of oxygen, head injury, or brain and meninges infection. A variety of muscular disorders are produced, with a spastic, jerky movement of the muscles being usual. Cerebral palsy is a very general classification, however, with different types having different symptoms in differing degrees, requiring different kinds of treatment. The usual symptoms may range from slight muscular incoordination to severe multiple handicaps which seriously hinder the child's ability to move around and learn. Muscle relaxants, anticonvulsant drugs, orthopedic surgery and corrective devices, early muscle training and exercise all can help considerably. The professional organization to contact is the:

United Cerebral Palsy Association, Inc.
66 East 34th Street
New York, NY 10016

Musclar dystrophy refers to a group of related muscle diseases that are progressively crippling because muscles are gradually weakened and eventually atrophy or wither away. It is not known what causes muscular dystrophy, and therefore there is no present cure. The disease is sometimes temporarily halted. Not all dystrophy forms are totally disabling. The basic mechanism of the disease is that muscles lose protein, with muscle fibers being replaced by fat and connective tissue. Finally, the voluntary muscle system becomes useless. It is suspected that heredity has something to do with the disease. No pain is involved and intelligence is not affected. The more active the victim is, the better he will be physically and mentally. More help can be received from the:

Muscular Dystrophy Associations of America, Inc.
1790 Broadway
New York, NY 10019

Paraplegia is paralysis of the legs, and in some cases, the lower part of the body. It is a form of central nervous system paralysis, the causative factors being varied. Treatment depends on the cause involved. More information can be obtained from the:

National Paraplegia Foundation
333 N. Michigan Avenue
Chicago, IL 60601

Tay-Sachs disease is an inherited neurological disorder. It is almost exclusively found in Jewish families whose ancestors came originally from a small area in eastern Europe near the Polish-Russian border. The disease usually shows up in an infant about six months of age when its development slows down and then deteriorates. The disease causes the body to store a material called glycalipid in the neurons of the brain and central nerv-

'ous system. This storing causes the neurons to swell, rupture, and die. Mental retardation, loss of motor ability, and eventually death follows by the age of two or three. Though there is no cure, the bright spot concerning this disease is genetic counseling. Laboratory tests have now been developed that can determine which individuals are carriers of Tay-Sachs disease. An individual has to inherit a defective gene for Tay-Sachs disease from *each* parent in order to have the disease. Therefore, if only one parent has the defective gene, the most the child can be is a carrier and not experience the disease. The professional organization concerned with this disorder is the:

National Tay-Sachs and Allied Diseases Association, Inc.
200 Park Avenue South
New York, NY 10003

20. Osteogenesis Imperfecta

Osteogenesis is a birth defect which has three characteristic symptoms, including brittle bones that fracture easily, deafness, and a bluish coloration in the white part of the eye. There may also be skeletal deformity due to imperfect formation and mineralization of bone. Treatment is limited and there is no known cure. More information can be received from:

Osteogenesis Imperfecta, Inc.
1231 May Court
Burlington, North Carolina 27215

21. Sickle Cell Anemia

This is an inherited disease, limited mainly to blacks, because it results from a genetic abnormality which began in people who lived in a wide geographic belt stretching across central Africa. If a person has one abnormal gene for sickle cell anemia, he will be a carrier but rarely suffer from any symptoms of the disease. A person who inherits a defective gene from each of his parents will have the disease.

The disease is characterized by abnormal hemoglobin, or red blood cells. The red blood cell in normal individuals is round. In the sickle cell anemia victim, the red blood cell has a variety of shapes caused by abnormal banding in the hemoglobin molecule. Symptoms include anemia, severe pain in the abdomen, joints, muscles and long bones, enlargement of the muscular part of the heart and other cardiac complications, and serious bouts with pneumonia and other respiratory infections. Other symptoms may include severe headaches, lethargy, convulsions,

paralysis, and even coma. The life of the victim is generally short-
ened.

　　There is no known cure for sickle cell anemia, but help in
treating and relieving the symptoms is available. Preventive care
is also being stressed. Continued research should pave the way
to a brighter future for sickle cell anemia victims. More information can be received from:

The Foundation for Research & Education in Sickle Cell Disease
421-431 West 120th Street
New York, NY 10027

Bibliography

Anderson, Fay Bennett, *Fay's Second Fifty.* Fact, August, Ga., 1975.
(This book gives activities for the young and the severely handicapped.)

Anderson, William, *Teaching the Physically Handicapped to Swim.* Faber, London, 1968.

Angel, Jurienal L., *Employment Opportunities for the Handicapped.* Simon and Schuster, New York, 1969.

Ayrault, Evelyn West, *You Can Raise Your Handicapped Child.* Putman, New York, 1964.

Barnes, Kenneth Haydon, *Language and the Mentally Retarded.* Worcester, 1970.
(This is a source book for teachers and parents on the teaching and studying of language for the handicapped.)

Berne, Eric, *The Games People Play.* New York, Grove Press, 1964.
(This book describes the psychology of human relations, dealing with concepts and games such as I'm OK, You're OK; Debtor, Alcoholic, Corner, Rapo, Uproar, etc.)

Birch, Jack W., and B. Kenneth Johnstone, *Designing Schools and Schooling for the Handicapped.* Thomas Publishing, Springfield, Ill. 1975.
(This is a guide to the dynamic interaction of space, instructional materials, facilities, educational objectives, and teaching methods.)

Blackwell, Robert B., and Robert R. Joynt, *Learning Disabilities Handbook for Teachers.* Thomas Publishing, Springfield, Ill., 1972.

Bremner, Robert H., *Care of Handicapped Children.* Arno press, New York, 1974.
(This book contains reprints of various articles on the care of the blind, deaf-blind, mentally retarded, and crippled children.)

Burton, Alma and Clea, *For They Shall Be Comforted.* (Salt Lake City, Deseret Books, 1964.
(Short messages of inspiration, hope, and comfort exressed for those who desire a clear understanding of the purpose of life, death, and the resurrection.)

Chapman, Frederick M., *Recreation Activities for the Handicapped.* Ronald Press Co., New York, 1960.

Doman, Glenn J., *What To Do About Your Brain-Injured Child.* Doubleday, Garden City, New York, 1974.
(This book discusses the care and treatment of the wide range of central nervous system-injured children.)

Dorward, Barbara, *Teaching Aids and Toys for Handicapped Children.* Council for Exceptional Children, 1960.

Downey, John A. and Niels L. Low, *The Child With Disabling Illness.* Saunders, Philadelphia, 1974.
(This book discusses principles of rehabilitation.)

Gearheart, Bill R., *The Handicapped Child in the Regular Classroom.* C.V. Mosby Co., 1976.
(This book discusses the possibilities of, and adjustments to, the handicapped child in a regular school program.)

Gordon, Sol, *Living Fully.* John Day Co., New York, 1975.
(This book is a compilation of addresses, essays, and lectures on family relations and the handicapped. It is a guide for young people with a handicap, and their parents, teachers, and professionals.)

Gordon, Thomas, *Parent Effectiveness Training.* New York, P.H. Wyden, 1970.
(Parents Effectiveness Training is a proven method to bring parents and their children together and to show parents how to help their children become mature, healthy, happy, and loving.)

Hart, Verna, *Beginning With The Handicapped.* Thomas Publishing, Springfield, Ill., 1974.
(This book deals with the care and treatment of handicapped children.

Heslinga, K., *Not Made of Stone.* Thomas, Springfield, Ill., 1974.
(This book discusses the sexual problems of handicapped people.)

Hill, Mary V., *Angel Children.* Horizon Publishers, 1973. pg. 44.
(The mother of a child who died in infancy of a congenital heart defect shares her feelings. She also presents the Latter-day Saint concept concerning the status of children who pass away before reaching the age of accountability. One chapter is devoted to the status of retarded children.)

Hofmann, Ruth B., *How To Build Special Furniture and Equipment for Handicapped Children.* Thomas Publishing Co., Springfield, Ill., 1970.

Johnson, Warren R., *Sex Education and Counseling of Special Groups.* Thomas, Springfield, Ill., 1975.

Jordan, William George, *The Majesty of Calmness.* Pyramid Publications, New York, 1966.
(A small, comprehensive presentation of the author's ideas on how people can have control over their lives by right thinking.)

Kate, Steven M., *The Special Educator's Index of Free Materials.* Journal for Special Educators of the Mentally Retarded, Center Conway, New Hampshire.

Katz, Alfred Hyman, *Parents of the Handicapped.* Thomas Publishing, Springfield Ill., 1961.
(This book discusses self-organized parents and relatives groups for treatment of the ill and handicapped children.)

Kimball, Spencer W., "The Right to Live". A tape recording, The Church of Jesus Christ of Latter-day Saints, 1975.

Kuaraceus, William C., and E. Nelson Hayls, *If Your Child is Handicapped.* Sargeant Publishing, Boston, 1969.
(This is a book of personal narratives.)

Lerner, Janet W., *Children With Learning Disabilities.* Houghton-Mifflin, Boston, 1976.
(This book discusses theories, diagnosis and teaching strategies for the child with learning disabilities.)

Lukine, Kathleen and Carol Panter, *Thursday's Child Has Far To Go.* Prentice-Hall, Englewood Cliffs, N.J., 1969.

Pearson, Paul, and Carol Ethun Williams, *Physical Therapy Services in the Developmental Disabilities.* Thomas Publishing, Springfield, Ill., 1972.

Riordan, Jennifer Talley, *They Can Sing Too.* Jenrich Associates, Leavenworth, Kansas, 1971.
(This book contains music and music therapy ideas and teaching for the deaf, brain damaged, mentally retarded, physically disabled, emotionally disturbed, or maladjusted, and those with speech problems.)

Rogers, Dale Evans, *Angel Unaware.* Fleming H. Revell Co.
(Dale Evans Rogers tells the story of her experience with a retarded child and how a tragedy became a triumph.)

Schattner, Regina, *Creative Dramatics for Handicapped Children.* John Day Co., New York, 1967.

Schultz, James D., *Special Education Teaching Games.* Denison, Minneapolis, 1975.
(This work is designed for the orthopedically handicapped, the mentally retarded, the emotionally disturbed, and slow learners.)

Schwarz, Berthold Eric, and Bartholomew A. Ruggieri, *You Can Raise Decent Children.* Arlington House, New Rochelle, N.Y., 1971.
(This book discusses child management and the parenting of handicapped children.)

Sill, Sterling, *That Ye Might Have Life.* Deseret Book Co., Salt Lake City, 1974.
(Sterling W. Sill describes how each person might make the most of life and be able to benefit from the promise of the Savior, "I am come that they might have life.")

Spock, Benjamin McLane, and Marion O. Lerrigo, *Caring for Your Disabled Child.* Macmillan, New York, 1965.

Stott, Denis Herbert, *The Parent as Teacher.* Lear Siegler/Fearon, Belmont, California, 1974.
(This is a guide for parents of children with learning disabilities.)

"When the Body is Imperfect," The Ensign Magazine, April, 1976, Vol. 6. Church of Jesus Christ of Latter-day Saints.
(This and several other articles in this issue describe the feelings and challenges of handicapped people.)

Thompson, Morton, *Recreation for the Homebound Person with Cerebral Palsy,* United Cerebral Palsy Association, New York, 1973.

Weiner, Florence, *Help for the Handicapped Child.* McGraw-Hill, New York, 1973.
(This book discusses rehabilitation programs for the handicapped.)

Index